# Unrebutted Stand A

COMES NOW **John Smithton: Doe**, the natural living flesh and blood man, a peaceful American National on the land, under oath, who states that the following information is of his own personal knowledge and belief.

## Contents

1. Declaration of Status ------------------ 3
2. Non-corporate Existence -------------- 7
3. Why Poverty Today? ------------------ 25
4. Usufructory Military Rule ------------- 33
5. The Untimate Delusion --------------- 43
6. The UCC-1 Finance Statement ------- 51
7. Remedy For Honor ------------------- 55
8. The Name of the Game -------------- 77
9. The Credit River Decision ------------ 89
10. Staying in Honor -------------------- 93
11. Regarding the IRS ------------------ 101
12. Redemption Demand --------------- 109
13. Note to Money Order Payee -------- 113
14. I Am Not The Name ---------------- 119
15. Banker's Testimony ----------------- 127
16. Affidavit of Truth ------------------- 143
17. Administration Notice -------------- 147
18. Acceptance for Value --------------- 151
19. The Crime of the Century ---------- 159
20. How did we give away our credit? --169

1

Copyright (c) 2018
by
David Everett: Robinson

**Maine Republic Email Report**
**https://mainerepublicemailreport.com/**

Please donate to help offset the costs of this Report
Please send me a note or two
http://www.paypal.me/DRobinson888

# AFFIDAVIT
## DECLARATION OF STATUS

STATENAME STATE    )
                   ) ss.
CountyName County  )

COMES NOW **John Smithton: Doe**, the natural living flesh and blood man, a peaceful American National on the land, under oath, who states that the following information is of his own personal knowledge, and belief.

**John Smithton: Doe** is not the fictional addressee "**JOHN SMITHTON DOE**".

**John Smithton: Doe** has Restored his Former Status from Being a Public United States citizen; a Federally-owned U.S. citizen as of March 9, 1933; nor a **Taxpayer/Bondman** put to Tribute September 8, 1936; to Being Once Again, A PRIVATE CITIZEN OF THE UNITED STATES OF AMERICA: A Private American Non-U.S. Citizen National Under Section I of the 14th Amendment to the Constitution for the United States of America.

### Declaration of Status
### John Smithton: Doe

### Pre-March 9, 1933, Private Citizen of the United States: American National

1. I, **John Smithton: Doe**, have released and disclaimed all legal obligations of suretyship and trusteeship in the Estate of "JOHN SMITHTON DOE" --- a StateName organization via a registered Certificate of Live Birth.

2. I, **John Smithton: Doe**, have rescinded all signatures of suretyship *nunc pro tunc, ab initio,* on behalf of Public U.S. Citizen JOHN SMITHTON DOE or any derivative of that NAME, effective from the filing date of said Certificate of Live Birth on Month, Day, Year, and provide the signature of agency as **Agent of Record, Executor, and Beneficiary**, without recourse.

3. I, **John Smithton: Doe**, have renounced, disclaimed, released, relinquished and abandoned the use of my former NAME, Public U.S. Citizen JOHN SMITHTON DOE, and have resumed the use of my Christian GIVEN Name, **John Smithton**, conferred on the day of my nativity, Month, Day, Year.

4. I, **John Smithton: Doe**, am a Pre-1933 Private American National Citizen defined by Section One of the Fourteenth Amendment to the Constitution for the United States of America, said status having been protected by the former, constitutionally-created civilian government ousted as of March 9, 1933; and during the provisional military government temporarily imposed by the congressionally approved and confirmed Proclamation 2040 of March 9, 1933 --- a Post-March 9, 1933 Private American Non-Citizen/National protected by Section One of the Fourteenth Amendment to the Constitution for the United States of America.

5. I, **John Smithton: Doe**, am NOT a state-created, federally-insured, statutory U.S. citizen in commerce or at war; nor am I the surety/trustee/registered agent/accommodating party for statutory U.S. citizen JOHN SMITHTON DOE or any derivative of that NAME. I am neither a Legal Fiction for the private Man created by God nor the statutorily-created, public, quasi-artificial PERSON created by the State.

6. I, **John Smithton: Doe**, am NOT, nor shall I ever consent to be publicly or privately the fiduciary/trustee for JOHN SMITHTON DOE, JOHN S. DOE, DOE, JOHN nor any other derivative of that NAME.

7. I, **John Smithton: Doe**, am the public **Agent of Record**, without recourse/without prejudice, and private Sole Beneficiary and Executor of the Estate and NAME of the Private Business Trust JOHN SMITHTON DOE; the Secretary of the Treasury of the United States being its fiduciary/trustee.

8. I act in accordance with the following U.S. Supreme Court case: -- **Hale v. Henkel**.

*"The individual may stand upon his constitutional rights as a citizen. He is entitled to carry on his private business in his own way. His power to contract is unlimited. He owes no such duty [to submit his books and papers for an examination] to the State, since he receives nothing therefrom, beyond the protection of his life and property. His rights are such as existed by the law of the land [Common Law] long antecedent to the organization of the State, and can only be taken from him by due process of law and in accordance with the Constitution. Among his rights are a refusal to incriminate himself, and the immunity of himself and his property from arrest or seizure except under a warrant of the law. He owes nothing to the public so long as he does not trespass upon their rights."* -- **Hale v. Henkel**, 201 U.S. 43 at 47 (1905).

Further Affiant Sayeth Not.

*All Rights Reserved*

/s/_____**John Smithton Doe**_____

**John Smithton: Doe,** StateName
National
Pre-March 9, 1933 Private American
National Citizen
Post-March 9, 1933 Private
American Non-Citizen/National
Private Resident of the Maine
Republic
Agent of Record without recourse/
without prejudice for
JOHN SMITHTON DOE
Sole Beneficiary and Executor for
the Estate and NAME of:
JOHN SMITHTON DOE, Ens legis
c/o Address
Zip City, State
nickname@emailaddress.net

*Subscribed To And Sworn To Before God [Titus 1:2] this XX.day of Month 20XX*

*Acknowledgement By Publication*

# AFFIDAVIT
## NON-CORPORATE EXISTENCE

STATENAME STATE  )
                                  ) ss.
CountyName County  )

COMES NOW **John Smithton: Doe**, the natural living flesh and blood man, a peaceful American National on the land, under oath, who states that the following information is of his own personal knowledge, and belief.

    Be it known to all courts, governments, and parties, that I, **John Smithton: Doe**, am a natural, freeborn Sovereign, without subjects. I am neither subject to any entity anywhere, nor is any entity subject to me. I neither dominate anyone, nor am I dominated.
    My authority for this statement is the same as it is for all free Sovereigns everywhere: the age-old, timeless, and universal respect for the intrinsic rights, property, freedoms, and responsibilities of the Sovereign Individual.
    I am not a "person" when such term is defined in statutes of the United States or statutes of the several states when such definition includes artificial entities. I refuse to be treated as a federally or state created entity that is only capable of exercising certain rights, privileges, or immunities as specifically granted by federal or state governments.
    I voluntarily choose to comply with the man-made laws which serve to bring harmony to society, but no such laws, nor their enforcers, have any authority over me. I am not in any jurisdiction, for I am not of subject status.
    Consistent with the eternal tradition of natural common law, unless I have harmed or violated someone

or their property, I have committed no crime; and am therefore not subject to any penalty.

I act in accordance with the following U.S. Supreme Court case: **Hale v. Henkel**, 201 U.S. 43 at 47 (1905) which states:

> "The individual may stand upon his constitutional rights as a citizen. He is entitled to carry on his private business in his own way. His power to contract is unlimited. He owes no such duty [to submit his books and papers for an examination] to the State, since he receives nothing therefrom, beyond the protection of his life and property. His rights are such as existed by the law of the land [Common Law] long antecedent to the organization of the State, and can only be taken from him by due process of law, and in accordance with the Constitution. Among his rights are a refusal to incriminate himself, and the immunity of himself and his property from arrest or seizure except under a warrant of the law. He owes nothing to the public so long as he does not trespass upon their rights."

Thus, be it known to all, that I reserve my natural common law right to not be compelled to perform under any contract that I did not enter into knowingly, voluntarily, and intentionally.

And furthermore, I do not accept the liability associated with the compelled and pretended "benefit" of any hidden or unrevealed contract or commercial agreement.

As such, the hidden or unrevealed contracts that supposedly create obligations to perform, for persons of subject status, are inapplicable to me, and are null and void. If I have participated in any of the supposed "benefits" associated with these hidden contracts,

I have done so under duress, for lack of any other practical alternative. I may have received such "benefits" but I have not accepted them in a manner that binds me to anything.

Any such participation does not constitute "acceptance" in contract law, because of the absence of full disclosure of any valid "offer," and voluntary consent, without mis-representation or coercion, under contract law. Without a valid voluntary offer and acceptance, knowingly entered into by both parties, there is no "meeting of the minds", and therefore no valid contract. Any supposed "contract" is therefore void, *ab initio* [from the beginning].

From my age of consent to the date affixed below, I have never signed a contract knowingly, willingly, intelligently, and voluntarily whereby I have waived any of my natural common law rights, and, as such, Take Notice that I revoke, cancel, and make void *ab initio* my signature on any and all contracts, agreements, forms, or any instrument which may be construed in any way to give any agency or department of any federal or state government authority, venue, or jurisdiction over me.

This position is in accordance with the U.S. Supreme Court decision of **Brady v. U.S.**, 379 U.S. 742 at 748 (1970):

> "Waivers of Constitutional Rights not only must be voluntary, they must be knowingly intelligent acts, done with sufficient awareness of the relevant circumstances and consequences."

Typical examples of such compelled and pretended "benefits" are:

1. **The use of Federal Reserve Notes to discharge my debts.** I have used these only because in America, there is none other widely recognized currency.

2. **The use of a bank account**, with my signature on the bank signature card. If there is any hidden contract behind the bank signature card, my signature thereon gives no validity to it. The signature is only for verification of identity. I can not be obligated to fulfill any hidden or unrevealed contract whatsoever, due to the absence of full disclosure and voluntary consent.

Likewise, my use of the bank account thereof is due to the absence of a bank not associated with the Federal Reserve system. In general, people have been prevented from issuing their own currencies, and such prevention is in violation of the United States Constitution. Were there an alternative, I would be happy to use it. To not use any bank at all is impossible or very difficult, as most everyone knows, in today's marketplace.

3. **The use of a Social Security number.** The number normally assigned to persons of subject status, I use exceptionally, under duress, only because of the extreme inconvenience of operating without one in today's marketplace, where it is requested by banks, employers, lenders, and many other government agencies and businesses. My reason for using it is not because I wish to participate in the Social Security system as it is presently structured. Let it be known that I use the Social Security number assigned to me for information purposes only.

4. **The use of a driver's license.** As a free Sovereign, there is no legal requirement for me to have such a license for travelling in my car. Technically, the unrevealed legal purpose of driver's licenses is commercial in nature. Since I don't carry passengers for hire, there is no law requiring me to have a license to travel for my own pleasure and that of my family and friends. However, because of the lack of education of police officers on this matter, should I be stopped for any reason and found to be without a license, it is likely

I would be ticketed and fined, or obligated to appear in court. Therefore, I carry a license, under duress, to avoid extreme inconvenience.

5. **State plates on my car.** Similarly, even though my car does not, technically, fit the legal definition of a "motor vehicle," which is used for commercial purposes, nevertheless, I have registered it with the state and carry the state plates on it, because to have any other plates or no plates at all, causes me to run the risk of police officer harassment and extreme inconvenience.

6. **Past tax returns filed.** Any tax returns I may have filed in the past, were filed due to the unlawful atmosphere of intimidation and fear created by the Internal Revenue Service (IRS), and the local assessor's office; not because there is any law requiring me to do so. Once I discovered that the IRS and other tax agencies have been misinforming the public, I have felt it is my responsible duty to society to terminate my voluntary participation. Because such returns were filed under Threat, Duress, and Coercion (TDC), and no two-way contract was ever signed with full disclosure, there is nothing in any past filing of returns or payments that created any valid contract. Therefore, no legal obligation on my part was ever created.

7. **Birth Certificate.** The fact that a birth certificate was granted to me by a local hospital or government agency when I entered this world, is irrelevant to my Sovereignty. No status, high or low, can be assigned to another person through a piece of paper, without the recipient's full knowledge and consent. Therefore, such a piece of paper provides date and place information only. It indicates nothing about jurisdiction, nothing about property ownership, nothing about rights, and nothing about subject status. The only documents that can have any legal meaning, as it concerns my status in society, are those which I have signed as an adult, with full knowledge and consent, free from misrepre-

sentation or coercion of any kind.

8. **Marriage license.** The acquisition of a marriage license is now being revealed as being necessary only for slaves. The act of a Sovereign such as myself obtaining such a license, through social custom and ignorance of law, has no legal effect in changing my status. This is because any such change in status, if any may be supposed to occur, could happen only through a hidden and unrevealed contract or statute. Since no hidden, unrevealed, and undisclosed information, if such exists, cannot be lawfully held to be binding, it is null and void.

9. **Children in public school.** The attendance of my children in government-supported "public" schools or government-controlled "private" schools does not create any legal tax obligation for me, nor any other legal obligation, because I never signed a contract agreeing to such obligation for the supposed "privilege" of public school attendance.

If any of my children have attended government supported "public" or controlled "private" schools, such was done under duress and not out of free will. Be it known that I regard "compulsory state education" as a violation of the **13th Amendment** to the U.S. Constitution, which states in relevant part:

> "Neither slavery nor involuntary servitude, except as a punishment for crime whereof the party shall have been duly convicted, shall exist within the United States, or any place subject to their jurisdiction."

10. **Declaration of Citizenship.** Any document I may have ever signed, in which I answered "yes" to the question, "Are you a U.S. citizen?" - cannot be used to compromise my status as a Sovereign, nor obligate me to perform in any manner. This is because without

full written disclosure of the definition and consequences of such supposed "citizenship," provided in a document bearing my signature given freely without misrepresentation or coercion, there can be no legally binding contract.

**I am not a "United States" citizen subject to its jurisdiction.** The United States is an entity created by the U.S. Constitution with jurisdiction as described on the following pages of this Affidavit. I am not a "resident of", an "inhabitant of", a "franchise of", a "subject of", a "ward of", the "property of", the "chattel of", or "subject to the jurisdiction of" any corporate federal government, corporate state government, corporate county government, corporate city government, or corporate municipal body politic created under the authority of the U.S. Constitution. I am not subject to any legislation, department, or agency created by such authorities, nor to the jurisdiction of any employees, officers, or agents deriving their authority therefrom.

Further, I am not a subject of the Administrative and Legislative Article IV Courts of the several states, or Article I Courts of the United States, or bound by precedents of such courts, deriving their jurisdiction from said authorities.

Take Notice that I hereby revoke, cancel, and make void *ab initio* any such instrument or any presumed election made by any of the several states or the United States government or any agency or department thereof, that I am nor ever have voluntary elected to be treated as a United States citizen subject to its jurisdiction, or a resident of any territory, possession, instrumentality, or enclave under the sovereignty or exclusive jurisdiction of any of the several states, or of the United States as defined in the U.S. Constitution in Article I, Section 8, Clause 17 and Article IV, Section 3, Clause 2.

11. **Past voter registration.** Similarly, since no obligation to perform in any manner was ever revealed in print, as part of the requirements for the supposed "privilege" to vote for government officials, any such registration on my part cannot be legal evidence of any obligation to perform.

Likewise, I have granted NO jurisdiction over me, to any political office. It is my inherent right to vote on elections or issues that I feel affect all of society; NOT because I need anyone to rule over me. On the contrary - I have used the voting process only to instruct my public servants what a Citizen and Sovereign would like to be done.

12. **Use of the 2-letter state code and zip code.** My use of the 2-letter state code and zip code in my "address", which is secretly codified to indicate United States "federal zone" jurisdiction, has no effect whatsoever on my Sovereign status. Simply by receiving or sending "mail" through a quasi-federal messenger service, the postal service, at a location indicated with a 2-letter state code and zip code, cannot place me under federal jurisdiction or obligation. Such a presumption would be ludicrous. I use these codes only for the purposes of information and making it more efficacious for the U.S. Postal Service to deliver my mail.

13. **Use of semantics.** There are some immature people with mental imbalances, such as the craving to dominate other people, who masquerade as "government." Just because they alter definitions of words in the law books to their supposed advantage, doesn't mean I accept those definitions. The fact that they define the words "person", "address", "mail", "resident", "motor vehicle", "driving", "passenger", "employee", "income", and many others, in ways different from the common usage, so as to be associated with a subject or slave status, means nothing in real life. Because the courts have become entangled in the game of

semantics, be it known to all courts and all parties, that if I have ever signed any document or spoken any words on record, using words defined by twists in the law books different from the common usage, there can be no effect whatsoever on my Sovereign status in society thereby, nor can there be created any obligation to perform in any manner, by the mere use of such words. Where the meaning in the common dictionary differs from the meaning in the law dictionary, the meaning in the common dictionary prevails, because it is more trustworthy.

14. **Compelled and supposed "benefits".** Such compelled and supposed "benefits" include, but are not limited to, the aforementioned typical examples. My use of such alleged "benefits" is under duress only, and is with full reservation of all my common law rights. I have waived none of my intrinsic rights and freedoms by my use thereof. Furthermore, my use of such compelled "benefits" may be temporary, until better alternatives become available, practical, and widely recognized.

## FEDERAL JURISDICTION

It is further relevant to this Affidavit that any violation of my Rights, Freedom or Property by the U.S. federal government, or any agent thereof, would be an illegal and unlawful excess, clearly outside the limited boundaries of federal jurisdiction. My understanding is that the jurisdiction of the U.S. federal government is defined by **Article I, Section 8, Clause 17** of the U.S. Constitution, quoted as follows:

> "The Congress shall have the power . . . To exercise exclusive legislation in all cases whatsoever, over such district (NOT EXCEEDING TEN MILES SQUARE) as may, by cession of particular states

and the acceptance of Congress, become the seat of the Government of the United States, [District of Columbia] and to exercise like authority over all places purchased by the consent of the legislature of the state in which the same shall be, for the Erection of Forts, Magazines, Arsenals, dock yards and other needful Buildings; And, To make all laws which shall be necessary and proper for carrying into Execution the foregoing Powers..."

and **Article IV, Section 3, Clause 2**:

"The Congress shall have the Power to dispose of and make all needful Rules and Regulations respecting the Territory or other Property belonging to the United States; and nothing in this Constitution shall be so construed as to Prejudice any Claims of the United States, or of any particular State."

The definition of the "United States" being used here, then, is limited to its territories:

1) The District of Columbia
2) Commonwealth of Puerto Rico
3) U.S. Virgin Islands
4) Guam
5) American Samoa
6) Northern Mariana Islands
7) Trust Territory of the Pacific Islands
8) Military bases within the several states
9) Federal agencies within the several states

The definition does not include the several states themselves, as is confirmed by the following two cites:

"We have in our political system a Government

of the United States and a government [governments] of each of the several States. Each one of these governments is distinct from the others, and each has citizens of its own who owe it allegiance, and whose rights, within its jurisdiction, it must protect. The same person may be at the same time a citizen of the United States and a Citizen of a State, but his rights of citizenship under one of these governments will be different from those he has under the other." - Slaughter House Cases **United States vs. Cruikshank**, 92 U.S. 542 (1875).

"THE UNITED STATES GOVERNMENT IS A FOREIGN CORPORATION WITH RESPECT TO A STATE." [emphasis added] **Volume 20: Corpus Juris Sec. §1785: NY re: Merriam** 36 N.E. 505 1441 S.Ct.1973, 41 L.Ed.287.

This is further confirmed by the following quote from the Internal Revenue Service:

Federal jurisdiction "includes the District of Columbia, the Commonwealth of Puerto Rico, the Virgin Islands, Guam, and American Samoa." - **Internal Revenue Code Section 312(e)**.

In legal terminology, the word "includes" means "is limited to."
When referring to this "District" United States, the Internal Revenue Code uses the term "WITHIN" the United States. When referring to the several States, the Internal Revenue Code uses the term "WITHOUT" the United States.
Dozens, perhaps hundreds, of court cases prove that federal jurisdiction is limited to the few federal territory areas above indicated. For example, in two

Supreme Court cases, it was decided:

> "The laws of Congress in respect to those matters do not extend into the territorial limits of the states, but have force only in the District of Columbia, and other places that are within the exclusive jurisdiction of the national government." **Caha v. United States**, 152 U.S., at 215.

> "We think a proper examination of this subject will show that the United States never held any municipal sovereignty, jurisdiction, or right of soil in and to the territory, of which Alabama or any of the new States were formed..."

> "[B]ecause, the United States have no constitutional capacity to exercise municipal jurisdiction, sovereignty, or eminent domain, within the limits of a State or elsewhere, except in the cases in which it is expressly granted..."

> "Alabama is therefore entitled to the sovereignty and jurisdiction over all the territory within her limits, subject to the common law." **Pollard v. Hagan**, 44 U.S. 221, 223, 228, 229.

Likewise, Title 18 of the United States Code at §7 specifies that the "territorial jurisdiction" of the United States extends only <u>outside</u> the boundaries of lands belonging to any of the several States.

Therefore, in addition to the fact that no unrevealed federal contract can obligate me to perform in any manner without my fully informed and uncoerced consent, likewise, no federal statutes or regulations apply to me or have any jurisdiction over me. I hereby affirm that I do not reside or work in any federal territory of the "District" United States, and therefore no U.S. federal government statutes or regulations have any authority over me.

## POWERS AND CONTRACTUAL OBLIGATIONS OF UNITED STATES AND STATE GOVERNMENT OFFICIALS

All United States and State government officials are hereby put on notice that I expect them to have recorded valid Oaths of Office in accordance with the **U.S. Constitution, Article VI**:

"The Senators and Representatives before mentioned, and the members of the several State Legislatures, and all executive and judicial officers, both of the United States and of the several States, shall be bound by oath or affirmation to support this Constitution..."

I understand by their Oaths of Office that all U.S. and State government officials are contractually bound by the U.S. Constitution as formulated by its framers, and not as "interpreted," subverted, or corrupted by the U.S. Supreme Court or other courts.
According to the **9th Amendment** to the U.S. Constitution:

"The enumeration in the Constitution of certain rights shall not be construed to deny or disparage others retained by the people."

and the **10th Amendment** to the U.S. Constitution:

"The powers not delegated to the United States

by the Constitution, nor prohibited by it to the States, are reserved to the States respectively, or to the people."

Thus, my understanding from these Amendments is that the powers of all U.S. and State government officials are limited to those specifically granted by the U.S. Constitution.

I further understand that any laws, statutes, ordinances, regulations, rules, and procedures contrary to the U.S. Constitution, as written by its framers, are null and void, as expressed in the **Sixteenth American Jurisprudence, Second Edition, Section 177**:

"The general misconception is that any statute passed by legislators bearing the appearance of law constitutes the law of the land. The U.S. Constitution is the supreme law of the land, and any statute, to be valid, must be in agreement. It is impossible for both the Constitution and a law violating it to be valid; one must prevail. This is succinctly stated as follows:

'The general rule is that an unconstitutional statute, though having the form and name of law, is in reality no law, but is wholly void, and ineffective for any purpose; since unconstitutionality dates from the time of its enactment, and not merely from the date of the decision so branding it. An unconstitutional law, in legal contemplation, is as inoperative as if it had never been passed. Such a statute leaves the question that it purports to settle just as it would be had the statute not been enacted.'

'Since an unconstitutional law is void, the general principles follow that it imposes no duties, confers no right, creates no office, bestows no power or authority on anyone, affords no

protection, and justifies no acts performed under it...'
'A void act cannot be legally consistent with a valid one. An unconstitutional law cannot operate to supersede any existing valid law. Indeed, insofar as a statute runs counter to the fundamental law of the land, it is superseded thereby.'
'No one is bound to obey an unconstitutional law and no courts are bound to enforce it.'"

and as expressed once again in **Article VI of the U.S. Constitution**:

"This Constitution, and the laws of the United States which shall be made in pursuance thereof; and all treaties made, or which shall be made, under the authority of the United States, shall be the supreme law of the land; and the judges in every State shall be bound thereby, anything in the Constitution or laws of any State to the contrary notwithstanding."

All U.S. and State government officials are therefore hereby put on notice that any violations of their contractual obligations to act in accordance with their U.S. Constitution, may result in prosecution to the full extent of the law, as well as the application of all available legal remedies to recover damages suffered by any parties damaged by any actions of U.S. and State government officials in violation of the U.S. Constitution.

## REVOCATION OF POWER OF ATTORNEY

Furthermore, I hereby revoke, rescind, and make void *ab initio,* all powers of attorney, in fact or otherwise, implied in law or otherwise, signed either by me or anyone else, as it pertains to the Social Security number assigned to me, **John Smithton: Doe**, as it pertains to my birth certificate, marriage or business license, or any other licenses or certificates issued by any and all government or quasi-governmental entities, due to the use of various elements of fraud by said agencies to attempt to deprive me of my Sovereignty and/or property.

I hereby waive, cancel, repudiate, and refuse to knowingly accept any alleged "benefit" or gratuity associated with any of the aforementioned licenses, numbers, or certificates. I do hereby revoke and rescind all powers of attorney, in fact or otherwise, signed by me or otherwise, implied in law or otherwise, with or without my consent or knowledge, as it pertains to any and all property, real or personal, corporeal or incorporeal, obtained in the past, present, or future. I am the sole and absolute legal owner and possess allodial title to any and all such property.

Take Notice that I also revoke, cancel, and make void *ab initio* all powers of attorney, in fact, in presumption, or otherwise, signed either by me or anyone else, claiming to act on my behalf, with or without my consent, as such power of attorney pertains to me or any property owned by me, by, but not limited to, any and all quasi/colorable, public, governmental entities or corporations on the grounds of constructive fraud, concealment, and nondisclosure of pertinent facts.

I affirm that all of the foregoing is true and correct.

I affirm that I am of lawful age and am competent to make this Affidavit. I hereby affix my own signature to all of the affirmations in this entire document with explicit reservation of all my unalienable rights and my specific common law right not to be bound by any contract or obligation which I have not entered into knowingly, willingly, voluntarily, and without misrepresentation, coercion, or duress.

FURTHER AFFIANT SAITH NOT.

*All Rights Reserved*

*/s/*_____**John Smithton Doe**_____

John Smithton Doe (c) LS, Authorized Representative/Attorney-In-Fact for:
JOHN SMITHTON DOE
c/o Address
Zip City, State
nickname@emailaddress.net

*Subscribed To And Sworn To Before God [Titus 1:2] this XX.day of Month 20XX*

*Acknowledgement By Publication*

# AFFIDAVIT
## WHY POVERTY TODAY?

STATENAME STATE    )
                                  ) ss.
CountyName County  )

COMES NOW **John Smithton: Doe**, the natural living flesh and blood man, a peaceful American National on the land, under oath, who states that the following information is of his own personal knowledge, and belief.

## Why Poverty Today?
## Do we know what poverty is?

Hello... One of these people are you. You had a long day at school... or was it shopping? Now you are home... Relaxed... Maybe you want to watch television.

These people live in constant fear of eviction... they had already been forced out of their home.

In some places people die... just so we can have more of our phones... children working as slaves.

The world is richer than it has ever been... and yet there seems to be more *poor* people than ever. Economies have been on the edge of a financial and economic precipice.

You are falling asleep... you're going to have a strange dream... it starts with this thought... if we want to make poverty history, we need to understand the history of poverty.

Your dream starts in a library full of books.

At the beginning of human history there was no inequality; virtually everybody was poor. Lack of infrastructure; massive disease; famine prevention; and people control; were the essential task of the Rulers. Some Secret Societies flourished. Others fell behind. We began to see poverty as something natural, something inevitable. **Nobody thought you could abolish poverty.** They simply accepted the fact that it is the way the world works.

Poverty is what makes the rich, rich. Power and wealth create a great divide.

The Industrial Revolution set the world on a course of science and technology, social housing, agricultural productivity, revolutionary movement, free market ideology.

It is now possible to make major dents in poverty. The People inspired by the Occupy Wall Street movement have the power to finally wrest control of our country from corporations and the wealthy, and return our country to a place **of the people, by the people, and for the people.**

Call me naive, but I believe that stuff that they taught us years ago in elementary school.

Over the last few weeks The Old Order has been shutting down occupied tent encampments around the country.

Well, they may have succeeded in forceably evicting peaceful protesters from some parks, **but you can't evict and idea whose time has come.** Brute violent force, whether perpetrated by the military or police in riot gear, can no longer contain people who are oppressed; whether it's over *there,* where countries are run by Dictators, or over *here,* where our country is run by Corporations.

The Internet, Social Networking, and Smart Phones, have forever changed the balance of power between the people and those who try to control them in their own narrow self interest.

Now that ordinary people can communicate with each other en-mass, without being filtered in real time, the people are truly powerful.

In just two short months Occupy Wall Street succeded in unmasking **America's dirty little secret** — that over the last three decades the income of the top 1% of Americans grew more than the income of the entire bottom 90%. Today the United States has the fifth largest spread between the rich and poor of every country in the world.

It is now common knowledge that 1% of America's population own up to 50% of the wealth!

The overall messages of Occupy Wall Street is that **this didn't happen by accident.** It's the result of tax policies, truce policies, subsidies, labor laws, regulations, or the lack thereof – and all of it has been done **in the narrow self interest of corporations** — many of which have privatized and socialized profits and costs.

Please pay attention. If you have eyes then see. If you have ears then hear. **We need to understand the cause of poverty today.**

— — —

Edward Mandell House was born in Houston Texas on July 26, 1858. He was an American diplomat, politician, and presidential advisor. He was known by the title Colonel House although he had no military experience. House had enormous personal influence with President Woodrow Wilson as his policy advisor, until Wilson removed him in 1919.

In the 1920's House strongly supported U.S. membership in the League of Nations and the World Court: the permanent Court of International Justice. In 1932 Colonel House supported Franklin Delano Roosevelt about joining the inner circle.

This one man, not mentioned in our history books, designed the first Shadow Government. He created the Counsel of Foreign Relations (CFR) with J. P. Morgan, John D. Rockefeller, Bernard Baruch, Otto Kahn, Jacob Schiff, and Paul Warburg. He formed the Trilateral Commission and the Bilderburg Group.

He set up the Federal Reserve Act of 1913 forming the twelve private U.S. branch banks of the Federal Reserve Bank which counterfeits money out of thin air and charges more than 700 million Percent Interest on it. He began the "New Era", the Great Depression of 1933, and the first World War.

Edward Mandell House was one of the most powerful and evil men in American history. He controlled all the presidents from Woodrow Wilson to Franklin Delano Roosevelt.

This evil man had a great disdain for the masses. He saw the people as stupid lazy slobs and referred to them as sheep going to the slaughter.

In a private meeting with Woodrow Wilson (President 1913-1921) Colonel House described his evil plan in the following words:

*"Very soon, every American will be required to register their biological property* [meaning his assets, his labor, and his given name] *in a National system designed to keep track of the people that will operate under the ancient system of the pledge.*

*By such methodology, we can compel people to submit to our agenda* [such as that of a mortgage company]*, which will affect our security as a chargeback* [of fiscal credit for the interest paid to the Federal Reserve for it to print and issue the official money of the corporate UNITED STATES, when instead, the U.S. Treasury could print and issue its own money free of charge] *for our fiat paper currency.*

*Every American will be forced to register* [for Social Security Insurance] *or suffer not being able to work and earn a living. They will be our chattel; and we will hold the security interest* [via hidden silent mortgage liens] *over them forever, by operation of the law merchant* [the international Uniform Commercial Code] *under the scheme of secured transactions* [such as mortgages, securities, and bonds].

*By unknowingly and unwittingly delivering to us their bills of lading* [the registrations of their Birth Certificates to be used as collateral for the debts of the dummy corporation: the federal UNITED STATES]*, Americans will be rendered insolvent and bankrupt, to forever remain economic slaves* [of the federal District of Columbia United States] *through* taxation, secured by the silently presumed pledge [of their assets, their labor, and their names; for the use of the public purse].

**They will be stripped of their** [constitutional] **rights and given a commercial value** [assigned to their registered Birth Certificates, now considered to be $1,000,000 [million] dollars as the nominal value of a human being's life energy, as collateral for the interest payments on the federal national debt] **designed to make us a profit and they will be none the wiser, for not one man in a million could ever figure out our plans and, if by accident one or two would figure it out we have in our arsenal plausible deniability.**

**After all, this is the only logical way to fund government, by floating liens and** [mortgage] **debt to the registrants** [of Social Security] **in the form of** [government bestowed] **benefits and privileges.**

**This will inevitably reap to us huge profits beyond our wildest expectations and leave every American a contributor to this fraud which we will call "Social Insurance."**

**Without realizing it, every American will insure us** [via bank bail outs and the graduated income tax] **for any loss we may incur** [via unchecked federal spending] **and in this manner, every American will unknowingly be our servant, however begrudgingly.**

**The people will become helpless and without any hope for their** [commercial] **redemption, and we will employ the high office of the President** [the Chief Executive Officer] **of our dummy corporation**

*[the Military Democracy United States in place of the Peaceful Republic]* **to foment this plot against America."**

Edward Mandell House was President Wilson's closest unofficial and unelected advisor.

Please pay attention. If you have eyes then see. If you have ears then hear. **We need to understand the cause of the poverty of today.**

*All Rights Reserved*

/s/_____**John Smithton Doe**_____

John Smithton Doe (c) LS, Authorized Representative/Attorney-In-Fact for:
JOHN SMITHTON DOE
c/o Address
Zip City, State
nickname@emailaddress.net

*Subscribed To And Sworn To Before God [Titus 1:2] this XX.day of Month 20XX*

*Acknowledgement By Publication*

# AFFIDAVIT
## USUFRUCT MILITARY RULE

STATENAME STATE   )
                  ) ss.
CountyName County )

COMES NOW **John Smithton: Doe**, the natural living flesh and blood man, a peaceful American National on the land, under oath, who states that the following information is of his own personal knowledge, and belief.

When the Representatives of the Southern States walked out of Congress, seceding from the Union at the start of the **Civil War** (*the war between the States*), and Congress adjourned *"sine dia"* (*without day to reconvene*), **Abraham Lincoln**, as the Commander in Chief of the Army of the Republic, under Military Rule (***military take-over***), ordered the government to continue according to the statutes of the newly established **Lieber Code** — Article 31 of which states:

> *"A victorious army appropriates all public money, seizes all public movable property until further direction by its government, and sequesters for its own benefit or of that of its government all the revenues of real property belonging to the hostile government or nation. The title to such real property remains in abeyance during military occupation, and until the conquest is made complete."* — Article 31, of the Lieber Code.

In other words:

Lincoln's Army took exclusive possession of all public

money (*in the U.S. Treasury*), seized the Title to all public movable property, and **set apart in a common Trust** all the revenues of the real property of State governments for the Army's benefit and the benefit of the United States. The Titles to such real property have remained in suspension, during the military occupation of the United States, and remain so today **until peace is declared.**

And to the property owners who did not flee the State, the commanding officer gave **"receipts"** to insure that the plundered owners would be **indemnified**.

> **"Private property, unless forfeited by crimes or by offenses of the owner, can be seized only by way of <u>military</u> necessity, for the support or other benefit of the Army or of the United States."** — Part 38, of the Lieber Code.

We call this part of the **Lieber Code**, **"the usufruct clause"**. Why? Because **"usufruct"** is the right to *use, enjoy,* and *benefit from* property owned by someone else.

> **<u>Usufruct</u>:** — *the right of enjoying a thing, the property of which is vested in another, and to draw from the same all the profit, utility and advantage which it may produce,* **provided that it be without altering the substance of the thing**."

So who has the *conditional right,* in this case? Who has the right to *use, enjoy,* and *benefit from* something that someone else owns, **provided that it be without altering the substance of the thing**?

Lincoln's Army had the right to *use, enjoy,* and *benefit from* the property that it seized from the people through conquest. **"To the victor goes the spoils."**

> **Usufructuary:** ...the one who has the right and enjoyment of an usufruct...

The **five duties** of the **Usufructuary** according to the **Rules of Usufruct** in the **Lieber Code** are:

> 1. **"To make** an inventory of the things subject to the usufruct, in the presence of those having an interest in them.
>
> 2. **"To give** security for their restitution; when the usufruct shall be at an end.
>
> 3. **"To take** good care of the things subject to the usufruct.
>
> 4. **"To pay** all taxes and claims which arise while the thing is in his possession, as a ground rent.
>
> 5. **"To keep** the thing in repair **at his own expense**."

Now many of you who read this will begin to ask, *"Ok, this is all well and good for the (so-called) United States, but what about the rest of us?"*

Have no fear, the **"engineers"** of the **"system"** also thought of the rest of us, which why they had a little Convention in a place called **"the Hague"** in 1907 and from that convention came Article 55, which states:

> **"The occupying State shall be regarded only as administrator and usufructuary of**

*public buildings, real estate, forests, and agricultural estates belonging to the hostile State and situated in the occupied country. It must safeguard the capital of these properties, and administer them in accordance with the rules of usufruct."*

**Article 38** of **The Lieber Code** acknowledges that the *"occupational forces"* have a corresponding duty to **not alter the lands or the** *"producers of the fruit"* **upon which it needs to survive**. This is how the Romans were able to *"conquer the world"*. They knew that if the lands were *"raped"* and *"torn asunder"* of the ability to produce what the army needed, the army was doomed. So, it would only take the **excess** for its needs and allow the lands and its *"inhabitants"* to keep **what they needed** to keep producing so the army would not starve, being so far away from *"home"*.

Lincoln's Army is the *"Usufructuary"* that had *the right to use, enjoy,* and *benefit from* what it seized from the people, **provided that it be without altering the substance of the thing**."

According to the **Rules of Usufruct** in the **Lieber Code**, the **Usufructuary** has the following five duties to do and maintain:

> 1. The **Usufructuary** (*the military government*) **must make** an inventory of *the people's property* subject to the usufruct, in the presence of those having an interest in them (*must publish that inventory list to all those concerned*).
>
> 2. The **Usufructuary** (*the military government*) **must give** security for the restitution of *the*

*people's property* at the end of the usufruct when peace shall be restored.

3. The **Usufructuary** (*the military government*) **must take** good care of *the people's property* subject to the usufruct.

4. The **Usufructuary** (*the military government*) **must pay all taxes and debt claims** which arise while *the people's property* is in its possession, *as a ground rent*.

5. The **Usufructuary** (*the military government*) **must maintain** *the people's property* in repair **at its own expense.**

Do not all roads lead to **"Rome"**?

It was nice of them to include us within the confines of this **"war"**. But how is the rest of the world **"included"**? Could it be that wherever the IMF [US Treasury; Fed Res] **"intervenes"** with a **"bailout"**; this **"system"** is then **"implemented"** ?

Why else would **"they"** be in Iraq, Iran, Afghanistan, and Pakistan? I'll bet if you look at **"history"**, you will find that IMF had **"loaned"** or **"given"** them some sort of **"assistance"**. Now, everyone can participate in the **"perfection"** that is **"the system"**.

You will also notice that all **Social Security** and **Birth Certificates** fall under the Department of Commerce and Agriculture (*agricultural estates*). Do you really think that this was by accident?

— — —

The **Birth Certificate Trust** that the federal Government created in my name when I was born (the **DAVID ROBINSON PUBLIC TRUST**) is a Public Vessel in Commerce which identifies the fictional **"PERSON"** that is using my given name as a part of the federal Municipal Trust.

This Trust is a **Roman Inferior Cestui Que Vie Trust** created by the Secretary of the Treasury of Puerto Rico, the Bankruptcy Receiver of the **United States of America, Incorporated**, *the failed government services corporation* Chartered in Delaware by the Roman Catholic Church.

As a result of the acts of this **"US Bankruptcy Trustee"**, all living Americans have been declared dead, *and are presumed to be lost at sea on the sea of commerce.*

All living Americans are classified in the **Internal Revenue Manual** (IRM 21.7.13.3.2.3) as *"infant decedents"* — *infants who have died*.

So when we notify the IRS of our correct status *as being alive* instead of as *"infant/decedent"* — and assign all our **reversionary interest** in the Social Security Trust Estate to and for the United States per Titles **12 USC 95a2** and **12 USC 95b** (*for "full acquittance and discharge"* of all our debts, we will be free of IRS control.

This is the Remedy guaranteed to us as a result of Congress issuing **fiat debt notes based upon our labor** instead of **real money of account based on silver and gold,** because the vast majority of us never agreed to this *"New Deal"*. We retain the full right of ownership and claim to our assets.

We are owed the **"re-venue"** (return) of our property without signing away any of our prerogatives and rights. This **"peace offer"** from the criminals running the **"US" Congress** is only a means for the perpetrators of crimes to avoid the consequences of their acts by presumably and tacitly securing our consent and a ***presumptive commercial contract*** allowing their abuse, and our own ***enslavement,*** to continue.

The United States of America (**minor**) never had any right to create the **JOHN QUINCY PUBLIC Trust** in the first place. So all assets of ***Roman Inferior Cestui Que Vie Trust*** revert to the entitlement holder, and must be returned to the ***entitlement holder*** (*"re-venued"*) ***free of debt*** and encumbrances accumulated by any false trustees or secondary beneficiaries.

Once it is clear that we are acting as ***living Americans on the land*** and are not agreeing to act as ***incorporated "things" ("PERSONS"),*** all members of the American Bar Association are ***obligated*** by the very Treaty that allows their presence on American soil ***to lend "aid and assistance" to us, — and the military forces are obligated to come to our defense.*** So unless you work for the Puerto Rican Commonwealth, and hope to be paid by them, you had all better do what's right.

The **JOHN QUINCY PUBLIC** Social Security Trust was created by the **Social Security Act of 1935** that says what it says. The Trust is coercive, bogus, and based on fraud; unfunded except by the labor and contributions of its victims.

**Articles 31 and 38 of the Lieber Code (*General Order 100*):**

**31. Holding Title in Abeyance** — all property is held in abeyance — including the **baby born on the battlefield** and the **income stream** from that **"asset"**. The Department of Defense takes the property **"in trust"** to hold **"in abeyance"** for **"safekeeping"**.

**38. Issuance of Indemnification Receipt** — the Birth Certificate. As peaceful civilian inhabitants on the land we are **"indemnified" from any cost and damage resulting from the actions of the US Army**.

Only **peaceful, living inhabitants** of the Domestic and Organic states have the **Civil Authority** to command the **Armed Forces of The United States of America Republic.** Only **WE** can require *the "US" Congress and the "President" of a governmental services corporation under contract to serve us,* to quit their criminal shenanigans — or be ousted like vermin driven from a storehouse.

All others by accepting **"citizenship"** of the **corporate UNITED STATES** — *including President Obama (now Trump) and ITS so-called U.S. Armed Forces* — have given up their right to say anything whatsoever to the *Armed Forces of our American Republic.*

*All Rights Reserved*

/s/_____**John Smithton Doe**_____

John Smithton Doe (c) LS, Authorized Representative/Attorney-In-Fact for:
JOHN SMITHTON DOE
c/o Address

Zip City, State
nickname@emailaddress.net

*Subscribed To And Sworn To Before God [Titus 1:2] this XX.day of Month 20XX*

*Acknowledgement By Publication*

WORLD'S HIGHEST STANDARD OF LIVING
There's no way like the American Way

# AFFIDAVIT
## THE ULTIMATE DELUSION

STATENAME STATE )
) ss.
CountyName County )

COMES NOW **John Smithton: Doe**, the natural living flesh and blood man, a peaceful American National on the land, under oath, who states that the following information is of his own personal knowledge, and belief.

King George and the so-called Founding Fathers were working hand-in-hand to bring the people of America to their knees, to install a Central Government over them and bind them to a debt that they could not pay.

First you have to understand that the UNITED STATES is a corporation that existed before the Revolutionary War. (See Republics v. Sweers, 1 Dallas 43, & 28 USC 3002 clause 15).

The UNITED STATES is not a land mass, it is a Corporation.

King George was not just the King of England, he was also the King of France. (Treaty of Peace, U.S. 8 Statutes at Large 80).

On January 22, 1783, Congress ratified a contract for the repayment of 21 loans that the UNITED STATES had already received dating from February 28, 1778 to July 5, 1782. Now the UNITED STATES, INC. owed the King money which was due to King George, via France, January 1, 1788, i.e., King George funded *both sides* of the American Revolutionary War.

The Articles of Confederation which were declared in force March 1, 1781, State in Article 12 that:

*"All bills of credit emitted, moneys borrowed, and debts contracted by, or under the authority of Congress, before the assembling of the United States, in pursuance of the present confederation, shall be deemed and considered a charge against the United States, for payment and satisfaction whereof the said United States, and the public faith are hereby solemnly pledged."*

The Articles of Confederation acknowledged the debt owed to King George. Now after King George's apparent loss of the Revolutionary War, that war is seen as nothing more than a move to turn the people into debtors to the King. For King George, the conquest was not then yet complete.

Now the loans were coming due, so a meeting was convened in Annapolis, Maryland, to discuss the economic instability of the Country under the Articles of Confederation.

Only five States came to the meeting, but there was a call for another meeting to take place in Philadelphia the following year, with the express purpose of revising the Articles of Confederation.

On February 21, 1787, Congress gave approval for a meeting to take place in Philadelphia on May 14, 1787, to revise the Articles of Confederation. Something had to be done about the mounting debt. Little did the people know that the so-called "founding fathers" were going to reorganize the United States, because it was Bankrupt.

On September 17, 1787 twelve State delegates approved the Constitution. The States now became Constitutors. A Constitutor, in civil law, is one who, by simple agreement, becomes responsible for the payment of another's debt. (Black's Law Dictionary 6th edition).

The States were now liable for the debt owed to the King, but the People of America were not, because they were not a party to the Constitution for it was never put to them for a vote. They are not a party to the Constitution even today.

On August 4th, 1790, an Act was passed Titled: "An Act making provision for the payment of the Debt of the United States." (1 U.S. Statutes at Large pages 138-178). This Act abolished the States and created Districts instead. Each District was assigned a portion of the federal debt.

The next step was for the States to reorganize their governments, which most did in 1790. This had to be done because the States needed to legally bind their people to the debt.

The original State Constitutions were never submitted to the people for a vote. So the State Governments wrote *new* constitutions and submitted *these* to the people for a vote, thereby binding the people to the debts that these *new* states then owed to Great Britain. The people became citizens of the state where they resided and, *ipso facto,* a citizen of the United States (dual citizenship).

A "citizen" is a member of a fictional entity and "citizen" is synonymous with "subject". What you think is a State is in reality a Corporation, in other words a

"Person" in law. (the State of Maine is a legal "Person"). *"The word 'person' does not include 'state'."* (12 Op Atty Gen 176).

There are now no States, just Corporations. Each and every body politic on this planet is a corporation. A corporation is an artificial entity, a fiction at law. Corporations only exist in your mind. They are images in your mind that speak to you. We labor, pledge our property, and give our children over to a fictional entity.

See "American Law and Procedure, Jurisprudence and Legal Institutions, Vol. XIII" by James De Witt Andrews LL.B [Albany Law School], LL.D [Ruskin University] from La Salle University. This book explains in detail the nature and purpose of these corporations. You will be stunned by what you read.

Article Six Section One of the U.S. Constitution keeps the loans from the King valid:

> **"All Debts contracted and Engagements entered into, before the Adoption of this Constitution, shall be as valid against the United States under this Constitution, as under the Confederation."**

Article One Section Eight clause Two states that Congress has the power to borrow money on the credit of [*the people of*] the United States. This was needed so the United States (which went into Bankruptcy on January 1, 1788) could borrow money. And then — because the States were a party to the Constitution — they became liable for its repayment.

The next underhanded move was the creation of The

United States Bank in 1791. This was a private bank that issued 25,000 shares of which 18,000 shares (72%, almost 2/3rds) were held by people in England. The United States Bank loaned the United States its money in exchange for interest bearing Securities of the United States.

So now the creditors of the United States, which included the King, wanted the Interest on the loans given to the United States, paid. So Alexander Hamilton came up with the great idea of taxing alcohol. When the people resisted, George Washington sent out the Miltia to collect the tax, which they did. This has become known as the Whiskey Rebellion. It was then, as it is now, the Militia's duty to collect taxes.

Question: How could the United States collect taxes from the people if the people were not a party to the Constitution? I'll tell you how. The people were then, and are now, debt slaves.

The United States belongs to the Founding Fathers, their posterity, and Great Britain. Ameirica is nothing more than a British Colonial plantation. It always has been. How many times have you seen someone in court attempt to cite the Constitution and the Judge tells him that he can't. It's because you are not a party to the Constitution. We are but Plantation slaves.

See Padelford, Fay & Co. v. The Mayor and Aldermen of the City of Savannah. 14 Georgia 438, 520:

> **"But indeed, no private person has a right to complain, by suit in court, on the ground of a breach of the Constitution, the Constitution, it is true, is a compact, but he is not a party to it."**

Article One Section Eight clause 15 states that it is the Militia's job to execute the laws of the Union. Then clause 16 states that Congress has the power to provide for organizing, arming, and disciplining the Militia, and for governing such part of them as may be employed in the service of the United States. In other words, the Militia is not there to protect you and me, it is the Militia's duty to collect our substance.

All the Constitution did was set up a Military Government to guard the King's commerce and make us Plantation slaves.

The "Treaty of Amity, Commerce and Navigation" (8 U.S. statutes at large 116-132) was signed on November 19th, 1794, twelve years after the War. Article 2 of the Treaty states that the King's Troops were still occupying the United States in 1794. Being the nice King that he was, he decided that the troops would return to England by June 1st, 1796, 20 years after the Declaration of Independence of 1776.

The troops were on American soil because the King wanted them here.

Many people tend to blame the Jews for our problems, but they too are, for the most part, also slaves. Jewish Law does, however, govern the entire world, as found in Jewish Law by Manachem Elon, Deputy President Supreme Court of Israel, to wit:

> **"Everything in the Babyonion Talmud is binding on all Israel. Every town and country must follow all customs, give effect to the decrees, and carry out the enactments of the Talmud Sages because the entire Jewish people accepted everything con-**

*tained in the Talmud. The Sages who adopted the enactments and decrees, instituted the practices, rendered the decisions, and derived the laws, constituted all or most of the Sages of Israel. It is they who received the tradition of the fundamentals of the entire Torah in unbroken succession going back to Moses, our teacher."*

We are living under what the Bible calls "Mammon". As written in the subject Index of the Bible, "Mammon" is defined as "Civil law and procedure".

*All Rights Reserved*

/s/_____**John Smithton Doe**_____

John Smithton Doe (c) LS, Authorized Representative/Attorney-In-Fact for:
JOHN SMITHTON DOE
c/o Address
Zip City, State
nickname@emailaddress.net

*Subscribed To And Sworn To Before God [Titus 1:2] this XX.day of Month 20XX*

*Acknowledgement By Publication*

**2013-765907-5**
Recording District 500   UCC Central File
08/22/2013 02:35 PM   Page 1 of 1

## UCC FINANCING STATEMENT
FOLLOW INSTRUCTIONS (front and back) CAREFULLY

A. NAME & PHONE OF CONTACT AT FILER [optional]
anna-maria:riezinger

B. SEND ACKNOWLEDGMENT TO: (Name and Address)

Anna M. Riezinger
c/o Box 520994
Big Lake, Alaska near 99652

THE ABOVE SPACE IS FOR FILING OFFICE USE ONLY

1. DEBTOR'S EXACT FULL LEGAL NAME

1a. ORGANIZATION'S NAME: **ANNA MARIA RIEZINGER**

| MAILING ADDRESS | CITY | STATE | POSTAL CODE | COUNTRY |
|---|---|---|---|---|
| BOX 520994 | Big Lake | AK | 99652 | usa |

TYPE OF ORGANIZATION: a trust
JURISDICTION OF ORGANIZATION: The United States of America
ORGANIZATIONAL ID #: 5,000,000

2. ADDITIONAL DEBTOR'S EXACT FULL LEGAL NAME

2a. ORGANIZATION'S NAME: **Anna Maria Riezinger**

| MAILING ADDRESS | CITY | STATE | POSTAL CODE | COUNTRY |
|---|---|---|---|---|
| c/o Box 520994 | Big Lake | AK | 99652 | usa |

TYPE OF ORGANIZATION: a trustee
JURISDICTION OF ORGANIZATION: The United States of America
ORGANIZATIONAL ID #: 100,000,000,000

3. SECURED PARTY'S NAME

INDIVIDUAL'S LAST NAME: riezinger   FIRST NAME: anna   MIDDLE NAME: maria

| MAILING ADDRESS | CITY | STATE | POSTAL CODE | COUNTRY |
|---|---|---|---|---|
| c/o Box 520994 | Big Lake | ak | [99652] | usa |

4. This FINANCING STATEMENT covers the following collateral:

**DEBTORS are TRUSTS AND TRANSMITTING UTILITIES**

All property real and intellectual held by the FOREIGN SITUS TRUST dba Anna Maria Riezinger created by the WISCONSIN STATE BOARD OF HEALTH File Number 148-56-46606 and ANNA MARIA RIEZINGER an ESTATE TRUST operated by agencies of the United Nations dba UN is the real and intellectual property of the SECURED PARTY symbolized as anna-maria:riezinger representing the living woman described as Anna Maria of the House of Riezinger known as Anna Maria Wilhelmina Hannah Sophia Riezinger von Reitzenstein von Lettow Vorbeck-- heir and beneficiary and equitable title holder.

All the fictional names listed together with all similarly styled names regardless of punctuation are the property of the living woman represented symbolically as anna-maria:riezinger and described as Anna Maria of the House of Riezinger. See UCC 1 File 2013-751967-5.

FILING OFFICE COPY — UCC FINANCING STATEMENT (FORM UCC1) (REV. 05/22/02)

# AFFIDAVIT
## THE UCC-1 FINANCE STATEMENT

STATENAME STATE    )
                                 ) ss.
CountyName County  )

COMES NOW **John Smithton: Doe**, the natural living flesh and blood man, a peaceful American National on the land, under oath, who states that the following information is of his own personal knowledge, and belief.

After learning more of the law and discovering who I am in relation to the United States Corporation, I **Accepted my Birth Certificate For Value** in my proper **Birth-Given-Name** (John Smithton) as the **Secured Party Creditor** of my estate and executed a lien upon *the government-created-all-capital-letter Strawman-Name* (JOHN) claiming everything that I own and will ever own and control as Collateral, and filed a **UCC-1 Financing Statement** converting myself from a **Debtor to the United States**, to a **Creditor of the United States**.

By filing a **UCC-1 Financing Statement**, I became a **Creditor with standing in law** and acquired the ability to **"state a claim upon which relief can be granted"** and not have the fruits of my labor taxed.

Without a **UCC-1 Financing Statement**, everything I had was pledged to and owned by the State (as in true Communism). I merely had USE of the property and had to use that property in strict compliance with all the many *rules, regulations, and "use fees" (taxes)* established by the State.

By filing a **UCC-1 Financing Statement** I acquired control over my property and as **Secured Party Creditor** was released from government control and can now **live free** of taxation concerns.

The biggest benefit in my filing a **UCC-1 Financing Statement** is that I am no longer a slave. A slave is anyone who is **even to a degree** an involuntarily subject to the will of another — or who **surrenders himself** to any power of control.

The United States holds **the form** (*the title; the birth certificate; the piece of paper*) but not **the substance** (*the baby that was me*).

When I filed the Financing Statement signed by me as the **owner** (John), I became the **holder-in-due-course** of **the title** of the "Strawman Person" (JOHN).

Registering a Security Agreement has priority over most other interests claimed in the same thing.

As the **owner of my estate** I notified the Secretary of the Treasury that I was going to handle my own affairs in the future (*to the best of my understanding and belie*f). I did this via the **"Charge Back Process"** which included a private **Registered Bond Accepted for Value Birth Certificate** respecting the value extended thereby, which provides me with the opportunity and ability to **discharge commercial debts** via **mutual offset credit exemption exchange**.

*All Rights Reserved*

/s/_____**John Smithton Doe**_____

John Smithton Doe (c) LS, Authorized

                    Representative/Attorney-In-Fact for:
                    JOHN SMITHTON DOE
                    c/o Address
                    Zip City, State
                    nickname@emailaddress.net

*Subscribed To And Sworn To Before God [Titus 1:2]
this XX.day of Month 20XX*

*Acknowledgement By Publication*

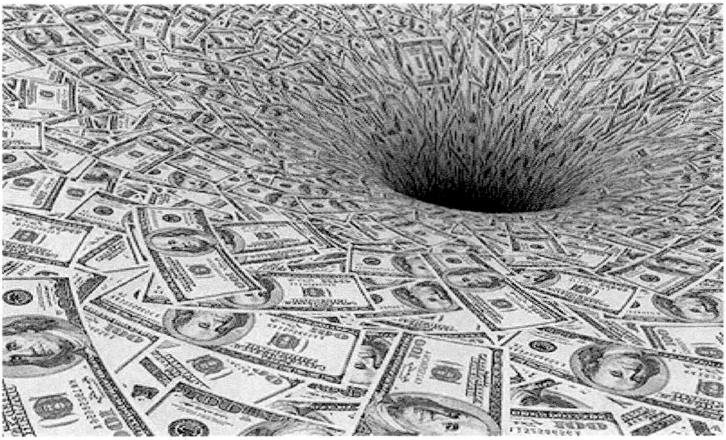

# AFFIDAVIT
## REMEDY FOR HONOR

STATENAME STATE      )
                     ) ss.
CountyName County    )

COMES NOW **John Smithton: Doe**, the natural living flesh and blood man, a peaceful American National on the land, under oath, who states that the following information is of his own personal knowledge, and belief.

Many who read **H.J.R. 192** ( House Joint Resolution 192 ) fail to comprehend its extraordinary significance. Its *six paragraphs* have done more to change the legal and financial landscape than perhaps any *six paragraphs* written prior to or since June 5, 1933. It represents no less than *the wholesale confiscation of the wealth of the people of America:* —the biggest theft in history. All property and labor was pledged to the International Banking Cartel in perpetuity (*forever*). Note that the word *"bankruptcy"* is *never* mentioned in this Resolution.

Considering the ease of obtaining incontrovertible evidence about the bankruptcy, it is shocking to learn that the majority of Americans are completely unaware that the bankruptcy ever occurred, how the American people were drawn into it, and how it became embedded in our lives.

And that Federal Reserve Notes are mere *promises to pay,* equivalent in value to paper *Monopoly money.* And that you don't have *actual title* to your vehicles and/or homes — you only get to use them — *if you pay your "use fees"* in the form of *registrations, licenses, and property tax*.

So complete in the comfort of their illusions are those who call themselves Americans.

If you create a system which is fraud from end to end, self-reinforcing and transparent, people won't even realize that it exists or how *they perpetuate* its existence.

— — —

In 1929, the *federal military social government construct* known as the *United States* entered the Great Depression. And most of the *major military economic powers* in the world at that time were also in Depression.

Americans were permitted to own gold, and their currency was backed by silver and gold. People could deposit their gold in a bank, and the bank would give them a paper note that they could use for withdrawing their gold when they so desired.

Due to the panic in the economic markets after the crash of 1929, people began withdrawing their silver and gold from the Federal Reserve Banks.

So President Hoover asked the Federal Reserve Board of New York to recommend how he should respond to this situation. So the Board adopted this resolution in response to President Hoover's request.

> **"Whereas, in the opinion of the Board of Directors of the Federal Reserve Bank of New York, the continued and increasing withdrawal of currency and gold from the banks of the country has created a national emergency."** *[from Herbert Hoover papers of March 3, 1933.]*

The Federal Reserve Board is stating here that *the run on banks is causing a "national emergency"*. But since the people's money was backed by gold, why would this cause a *national emergency* for people to hold the gold rather than the banks? And President Hoover later said this:

> **"This first contract of the moneychangers with the New Deal netted those who removed their money from the country a profit of up to 60 percent when the dollar was debased."** [Hoover Policy Paper, written by the Secretary of Interior and Secretary of Agriculture]

President Hoover is saying here that the insiders with inside knowledge had already removed their their gold from the country before the uninformed people began demanding the withdrawal of their gold from the banks. And since the banks didn't have the gold the people were demanding, the banks needed government protection.

So the Federal Reserve Board proposed that President Hoover issue the following **Executive Order** based on the **Trading with the Enemy Act of 1917**:

> **"Whereas, it is provided in Section 5(b) of the Act of October 6, 1917, as amended, that 'the President may investigate, regulate, or prohibit, under such rules and regulations as he may prescribe by means of licensure or otherwise, any transaction in foreign exchange and the export, hoarding, melting, or ear marking of gold or silver coin or bullion or currency."** [Herbert Hoover private papers of March 3, 1933]

**President Hoover** declined to issue the order, but when **Franklin Delano Roosevelt** was inaugurated as President, on **March 4, 1933**, he *requested* in his inauguration speech that Congress grant him **emergency powers, equal to those he would have in times of war,** to allow him to deal with the crisis.

The very next day, on **March 5, 1933,** Roosevelt issued **Proclamation 2038** requesting a **Special Session of Congress** beginning on **March 9, 1933,** to deal with the banking emergency. Then seven days later, on **March 16, 1933**, he issued **Proclamation 2039** to outline to the Congress the **emergency powers** he was requesting. This Proclamation had exactly the same *wording* as advised by the **Federal Reserve Board** but it had no *authority* until Congress met to give the President the *required* authority.

Some researchers speculate that the depression was engineered by the **international bankers** whom the **Federal Reserve System** represents. The **banker's** motive was to further consolidate their power. It is also speculated that the *federal military social government construct* known as the *United States* was told that it had no choice but to cooperate with the **Federal Reserve Board** *(and the international bankers)* or the depression would continue indefinitely *(political blackmail)*.

On the first day of the special session Congress approved **Proclamation 2039** which President Roosevelt then issued as **Proclamation 2040**.

> *"Whereas, under the Act of March 9, 1933, all Proclamations heretofore or hereafter issued by the President pursuant to the authority enforced by section 5(b) of the Act*

*of October 6, 1917, as amended, are approved and confirmed."* [President Roosevelt's Proclamation 2040]

And then, on the same day, Congress passed the following statute:

*"During time of war or during any other period of national emergency declared by the President, the President may, through any agency that he may designate, or otherwise investigate, regulate, or prohibit, under such rules and regulations as he may prescribe, by means of licensure or other wise, any transaction in foreign exchange, transactions of credit between or payments by banking institutions as defined by the President, and export, hoarding, melting, or ear marking of gold or silver coin or bullion or currency, by any person within the United States or anyplace subject to the jurisdiction thereof."* [Title 1, Sec. 2, 48 Statute 1, March 9, 1933, The Emergency Banking Relief Act of 1933]

This is exactly the same wording that was found in the **Trading with the Enemy Act of 1917** except that the exclusion *"except for transactions within the UNITED STATES"* has been deleted.

This Statute can be found in the United States Code as title **12 USC 95b**. Here is the current version of this Statute. Notice that the wording is almost identical to the wording found in the 1933 Statute shown in the paragraph above.

> **Section 95b. — Ratification of acts of President and Secretary of the Treasury under section 95a.**
>
> *"The actions, regulations, rules, licenses, orders and proclamations heretofore or hereafter taken, promulgated, made, or issued by the President of the United States or the Secretary of the Treasury since March 4, 1933, pursuant to the authority conferred by section 95a of this title, are approved and confirmed."* [Title 12 USC 95b]

This version says that the *authority* is granted in **12 USC 95a**. But if you look in the notes to that statute you will see that the original source authority is located in **"Oct. 6, 1917, ch. 106, Sec. 5(b), 40 State. 415"** and later in **"Mar. 9, 1933, ch. 1, title I, Sec. 2, 48 State. 1."** So *even now* the President has the authority that was originally granted in 1917 and was later modified in 1933 — **to include Americans as enemies of the United States.**

The present effect of this emergency power is that *all Americans* are now an included part of the **Trading with the Enemy Act as amended in 1933**. Since the bankers didn't have the gold to pay out, President Roosevelt used **Proclamations 2039** and **2040** — and title **12 USC 95b** — to create a banking holiday

> *"Bank holiday of 1933. Presidential Proclamations No. 2039, issued March 6, 1933, and No. 2040, issued March 9, 1933, temporarily suspended banking transactions by member banks of the Federal Reserve System. Normal banking functions were resumed on March 14, subject to certain*

> **restrictions. The first proclamation, it was held, had no authority in law until the passage on March 9, 1933, of a ratified act (12 USC 95b). The present law forbids member banks of the Federal Reserve System to transact banking business, except under regulations of the Secretary of the Treasury, during an emergency proclaimed by the President. 12 USC 95."** [Black's law Dictionary, 5th Edition]

The restrictions mentioned above are that the bankers had to be licensed before the banks could be reopened. A license is something that grants authority to do something that would otherwise be illegal. Trading or conducting business with the enemy (**with so-called Americans on assumed American soil**) was made an illegal activity **unless licensed by the State**.

> **"The Secretary of the Treasury will issue licenses to banks which are members of the Federal Reserve System whether national bank or state, located in each of the 12 Federal Reserve Bank Cities, to open Monday morning."** [President Roosevelt's papers]

Another provision passed on **March 9, 1933** gave **Federal Reserve Agents** the authority to act as **Agents of the U.S. Department of Treasury**. This seems strange since the non-federal **Federal Reserve System** is a privately incorporated business.

> **"When required to do so by the Secretary of the Treasury, each Federal Reserve Agent shall act as agent of the Treasurer of the United States or of the Comptroller of the Currency, or both, for the performances of**

*any functions which the Treasurer or the Comptroller may be called upon to perform in carrying out the provisions of this paragraph."* [48 Stat. 1,]

We've already seen that insiders had removed most of the gold from the banks before the people started demanding their gold (money) from the banks. The bankers didn't have the gold that the people were demanding so the bankers sought protection. In order to do this, the people were declared by statute to be the **Enemy of the United States** by the **Trading with the Enemy Act** as revised in 1933, to include them and to accomplish this. Congress then passed a statute that authorized fines and/or prison sentences if people didn't turn in their gold. This would be considered High Treason if the power used was not founded upon **the Law of Necessity** instead of true representative authority by a fully aware and informed people.

*"Whenever in the judgment of the Secretary of the Treasury, such action is necessary to protect the currency system of the United States, the Secretary of the Treasury, in his discretion, may regulate any or all individuals, partnerships, associations and corporations to pay and deliver to the Treasurer of the United States any or all gold coin, gold bullion, and gold certificates owned by such individuals, partnerships, associations, and corporations. ... Whoever shall not comply with the provisions of this act shall be fined not more that $10,000 or if a natural person, in addition to such fine may be imprisoned for a year, not exceeding ten years."* [Stat. 48, Section 1, Title 1, Subsection N, March 9, 1933]

So, not only were people not able to get their gold, but their gold was confiscated by the *federal military social government construct.* Since all the people's money was gold and silver certificates and all of it had to be turned in, *the people were left without any money of exchange in Law*.

> **"During this banking holiday it was at first believed that some form of script or emergency currency would be necessary for the conduct of ordinary business. We knew that it would be essential when the banks reopened to have an adequate supply of currency to meet all possible demands of depositors. Consideration was given by government officials and various local agencies to the advisability of issuing clearing house certificates or some similar form of local emergency currencies. On March 7, 1933, the secretary of the Treasury issued a regulation authorizing clearing houses to issue demand certificates against sound assets of the banking institutions. but this authority was not to become effective until March 10th. In many cities, the printing of these certificates was actually begun. But after the passage of the Emergency Banking Act of March 9, 1933 (48 Stat. 1), it became evident that they would not be needed because the act made possible the issue of the necessary amount of emergency currency in the form of Federal Reserve Bank Notes which could be based on any sound assets owned by the banks."** *[Roosevelt's papers]*

So President Franklin Delano Roosevelt's papers admitted that the **Emergency Banking Ac**t made it possible to issue *emergency currency* that was based upon the *so-called Assets of the Banks* rather than upon gold or silver (**removing the US from the <u>Gold Standard</u> and placing the US on the <u>Promissory Note Standard</u> instead).** The **"emergency currency"** was, and is, **"Federal Reserve Bank Notes"** which are the **<u>Promissory Notes</u>** used in America today.

— — —

Now we will see what was (and is) used to back up the **"Federal Reserve Bank Notes"**.

> ***"Upon the deposit with the Treasurer of the United States, (a) of any direct obligations of the United States, or (b) of any notes, drafts, bill of exchange or bankers acceptances acquired under the provisions of this Act, any Federal Reserve bank making such deposit in the manner prescribed by the Secretary of the Treasury shall be entitled to receive from the Comptroller of the currency circulating notes in blank, duly registered and countersigned."*** *[Emergency Banking Act of March 9, 1933, section 4, Public Law 89-719]*

On **June 5, 1933**, the House of Representatives passed **HJR 192,** a joint resolution of **Senate and House,** to **"Suspend The Gold Standard and Abrogate The Gold Clause",** which says in part:

> ***"That (a) every provision contained in or made with respect to any obligation which purports to give the obligee a right to require payment in gold or particular kind of coin or currency, or in an amount of money***

*of the United States measured thereby is declared to be against public policy; and no such provision shall be contained in or made with respect to any obligation hereafter incurred."* [House Joint Resolution 192, June 5, 1933]

Since this measure was passed as a joint resolution, it doesn't have the force of law. Notice that the resolution uses the term **"public policy"** that we frequently hear used today.

*"public policy. Broadly, principles and standards regarded by the legislature or by the courts as being of fundamental concern to the state and the whole of society."* [Black's Law Dictionary, 7th Edition]

. . . public policy is not the same as public law.

*"public law. The body of law dealing with the relations between private individuals and the government, and with the structure and operation of the government itself; ... A statue affecting the general public ..."* [Black's Law Dictionary, 7th Edition]

This is a rather **startling admission** on Congress' part. They are admitting here that what they are doing by refusing to pay the federal debt in gold is NOT according to **"public law"** but is rather a **"public policy"**.

So we see here that our money is no longer backed by gold (*even if it is only a public policy*). The *new money* is **Federal Reserve Bank Notes**. These notes are backed by **"direct obligations of the United States"** which are Treasury Notes. They are also backed by bank **"notes, drafts, bills of exchange, and acceptances."** This last group consists of notes that Federal Reserve member banks are holding on loans they had made to people and institutions. So the public and/or private debt instruments of the banks are considered Assets to be deposited in the U.S. Treasury in exchange for **"circulating notes"**. Excerpts can further prove this from the Congressional Record during the debate of the **Emergency Banking Act of 1933**.

[Mr. McPhadin] *"The first section of the bill, as I grasped it, is practically the War Powers that were given back in 1917. I would like to ask the Chairman of the Committee if this is a plan to change the holding of the security back of the Federal Reserve Notes to the Treasury of the United States rather than the Federal Reserve agent."*

[Mr. Stiggle] *"This provision is for the issuance of Federal Reserve Bank notes; and not for Federal Reserve notes; and the security back of it is the obligations, notes, drafts, bills of exchange, bank acceptances, outlined in the section to which the gentleman has referred."*

[Mr. McPhadin] *"Then the new circulation is to be Federal Reserve Bank Notes and not Federal Reserve Notes. Is that true?"*

[Mr. Stiggle] *"Insofar as the provisions of this section are concerned, yes."*

[Mr. Stiggle] *"From my observations of the bill as it was read to the House, it would appear that the amount of bank notes that might be issued by the Federal Reserve System is not limited (is unlimited). That it will depend entirely upon the amount of collateral that is presented from time to time from exchange for bank notes. Is that not correct?"*

[Mr. McPhadin] *"Yes, I think that is correct."*

— — —

It should be clear here that *the currency is no longer backed by gold* but by **promises to pay** on various debt instruments; i.e., loans to private individuals or businesses and the government. So there are no **hard assets** backing up the currency, *only* **promises to pay**. In the case of government loans, the collateral is the *"full faith and credit of the United States"*. This is very strong evidence that the federal government was bankrupt at that time. If it were not, the federal government would still be willing to pay its obligations *in gold* and the currency would still be *backed by gold*.

To whom does the federal government owe the money? The obvious answer is the Federal Reserve Bankers who hold the *"direct obligations of the United States"*.

The non-federal Federal Reserve is a private bank, it is not part of the government. The logical conclusion is that *the United States government is bankrupt* and the Federal Reserve is the Creditor of the federal UNITED STATES.

The transition from a gold backed currency to one that is not backed by hard assets was very swift. The Federal Reserve Board proposed it to their President, Herbert Hoover, but it took until a more acceptable agent entered the *military social construct* on March 3, 1933 before it was implemented into Law on March 9, 1933. This is very swift action indeed.

How can we account for such a repaid change in circumstances? We have *not* thus far uncovered any direct evidence of undue influence by the *international bankers* of the Federal Reserve. However, their position as Creditor to the UNITED STATES provides a plausible explanation of why things changed so very rapidly.

— — —

Let's now clarify the difference between **"real money of exchange"** (*backed by a hard assets*) and **"paper money of account"** as a money substitute. Federal Reserve Notes (FRNs) are nothing more than *promissory notes promising to pay the federal debt to the non-federal* Federal Reserve Bank (FRB) backed by UNITED STATES *treasury securities* (T-Bills).

The Federal Reserve Bank allows the *federal military social government construct* to create debt that causes inflation through the devaluation of the so-called currency. Inflation occurs whenever there is an increase in the *backing behind the "money of exchange"* (*i.e., promises to pay the federal debt to the non-federal Federal Reserve Bank*).

Inflation is an invisible form of taxation that irresponsible governments inflict on their subjects known as citizens. The Federal Reserve Bank has access to an unlimited supply of FRNs, The Federal Reserve Bank only pays for the printing costs of new FRNs.

There is also a fundamental difference between **"paying"** and **"discharging"** a debt. To pay a debt you must pay with value or substance (such as gold, silver, barter, or a commodity). With FRNs, you can only discharge a debt. You cannot pay a debt with a debt currency system. You cannot service a debt with a currency that has no backing in value or substance. *No contract in common law is valid unless it involves an exchange of "good and valuable consideration".*

So what does the *federal military social government construct* have to offer the Federal Reserve in payment of its debts?

> **"The money will be worth 100 cents on the dollar because it is backed by the credit of all the people of the Nation. It will represent a mortgage on all the homes and other property of all the people in the Nation." [Banker Patton, Congressional Record, March 9, 1933].**

We now see that the federal government has offered all of the private property of the people to its creditor, the non-federal Federal Reserve. The government has also offered the labor of the people of the nation. The IRS is used to collect money for the non-federal Federal Reserve (not for the government).

The *federal military social government construct* "hypothecated" all of the present and future *properties, assets, and labor* of their "subjects" to the non-federal Federal Reserve Bank.

> **"Hypothecate. To pledge property as security or collateral for a debt. Generally, there is no physical transfer of the pledged property to the lender; nor is the lender given title to the property; though he has a right to sell the pledged property upon default."**
> [Black's Law Dictionary, 5th Edition]

So, the *federal military social government construct* has pledged (*mortgaged*) our property as collateral to their Creditor, the non-federal Federal Reserve.

If you think that the only people who can mortgage property are the owners of the property you are correct. The implication here is that the *federal military social government construct* has taken over *controlling interest* in our property. This seems like a violation of the 5th Amendment to the *social compact contract* known as the U.S. Constitution, but it is not.

What *social compact contract Constitution* are you a part of? None.

The *federal military social government construct* continues to *rape and pillage* based upon your full faith and credit to continue to believe the following to wit: **"...nor shall private property be taken for public use without just compensation."** [from 5th Amendment]

You may wonder how you got roped into paying someone else's debts.

> **"The validity of the public debt of the United States...shall not be questioned."** [14th Amendment, section 4].

After passage of the 14th Amendment, everyone born in the so-called UNITED STATES became a 14th Amendment federal Citizen. As such they are held liable for the *"public debt of the United States"*.

In return for turning over all the property in the so-called *federal military social government construct* known as the United States, the Federal Reserve Bank agreed to extend it all the **Credit** (money substitute) it needed. So like any other debtor, the *federal military social government construct* had to **assign** collateral and security to **their** Creditors as a condition of the loan.

Since they didn't have any **assets**, they **assigned** the **private property** of their **"economic slaves"**, the so-called UNITED STATES Citizen, as collateral against the **un**-payable federal military debt. They **pledged** the **unincorporated** federal military territories, national parks, and forests, as collateral against the federal military debt as well.

In Summary, the *Federal Military Social Government Construct* is bankrupt. The Federal Reserve Bankers are the Fiscal Agents for the Creditor of the *Federal Military Social Government Construct*. All your property and labor have been **pledged** to pay the debts of the *Federal Military Social Government Construct*. You, as a **UNITED STATES Citizen**, are held **liable** for the so-called military Public Debt and as a service agent of the **fiscal agent of** the Federal Reserve Bank, since the Internal Revenue Service (**IRS**) is the collection agency for the Federal Reserve Bank.

— — —

### From HJR 192 of June 5, 1933

*"Every obligation, heretofore or hereafter incurred, whether or not any such provision is contained therein or made with respect thereto, shall be discharged upon payment, dollar for dollar, in any coin or currency which at the time of payment is legal tender for public and private debts."*

# Title 12 USC 95a2

**Title 12 USC 95a2 of the Emergency Banking Acts** (of 1862, 1864, 1865 and 1933) **presents a <u>Remedy</u> for the People of the United States of America.**

1. The 1917 Trading With The Enemy Act as amended in 1933 lists all Americans as enemy combatants; prisoners of war; unlawful combatants out of uniform being belligerent until we announce that our purposes and actions are peaceful in an expressed and positive way. [*By way of a personal Affidavit?*]

2. We are not at war. We are not warring with anyone. We are not belligerent.

3. We are not *U.S. citizens*. We are *non-resident aliens* of the *federal zone United States*. We are *non-citizen nationals* of the United States of America.

4. We are not a part of the *federal zone United States*. We are not at war with the *federal United States*.

5. We make no claim to Titles. The Birth Certificate is a Certificate of Title. The Name on it is a Title found on an Infant Registry Certificate which is not the name of an adult. The Adult must come forward and remit (return) that Birth Certificate to the federal United States. But most people are not doing this **remittance** that they should do (*the* **remittance** *under title* **12 USC 95(a)2**).

6. We need to pledge ourselves to the **Declaration of Independence** and become a party to this contract (not to the U.S. Constitution). The **Declaration of Independence** was declared three years **before** the United States Constitution was signed.

7. We must pledge to protect ourselves and all individuals in America (*and in the world*).

8. We are **non-combatant-non-belligerents** who surrender and assign all reversionary interest in our *STRAWMAN NAME* to the federal zone UNITED STATES *for full acquittance, discharge, settlement, and closure of our ESTATE NAME ACCOUNT* in reliance on title 12 USC 95(a)2.

9. We assume no liability for the debts of the corporate federal UNITED STATES, for we never consented to stand as surety for its debts.

10. We are in a *USUFRUCT* capacity and position.

11. We stand as the sole beneficiary of our individual *STRAWMAN ESTATE TRUST*.

12. In honor of all non-combative, non-resident, non-citizen, peaceful abiding women and men, *reversionary interest confirms that* **everything has been paid for** *per title 12 USC 95(a)2 to wit:*

*Section (2). Any payment, conveyance, transfer, assignment, or delivery of property or interest therein, made to or for the account of the United States, or as otherwise directed, pursuant to this section or any rule, regulation, instruction, or direction issued hereunder shall to the extent thereof be a full acquittance and discharge for all purposes of the obligation of the person making the same; and no person shall be held liable in any court for or in respect to anything done or omitted in good faith in connection with the administration of, or in pursuance of and in reliance on, this section, or any rule, regulation, instruction, or direction issued hereunder.*

13. By the use of this Rule, everyone can and will be tax-free. Whenever you receive a tax bill tell them that you are operating under title **12 USC 95(a)2** and relying on that law. This is all you have to say.

14. It is the same wording as the **Trading with the Enemy Act of 1917**.

15. The Estate is not ours. It's usufruct. We only use the assets that belong to the State for the **benefits** they bestow. **We must return the "reversionary interest" to the Source.** We must return the STRAWMAN-PERSON represented by **the birth certificate** to its Source by assigning our reversionary interest in the STRAWMAN NAME to that Source: the federal zone corporate UNITED STATES.

16. **It's all fiction. It's a Matrix. We are now Aware.**

— — —

If I (*as the government*) come and take from you by way of SEIZING things where you have no say so in the matter because I have the guns and force behind me in that which I claim is my right to do out of necessity under my War Powers, then how have you GRANTED me anything?

If you have not GRANTED some thing then you are not GIFTING it. But if you did GRANT something then you have not been SPOLIATED, because nothing was taken and seized from you if you voluntarily GRANTED it instead!

Now, since I am NOT a party to the Seizure, and NOT a GRANTOR or a GIFTER of anything and I have been SPOLIATED by such Seizure, then I am entitled to INDEMNITY from any and all CLAIMS against the *ESTATE NAME* — **for the HONOR OF THE NAME.**

Everything has already been done! Everything has already been seized. *And the **delivery of property or interest therein** (titles, deeds, registrations, etc.) **has been made to or for the account of the UNITED STATES** out of necessity to support the UNITED STATES and its Army by way of that declared state of National Emergency (bankruptcy) in 1933 via the War Powers, the Rules of War on land, and General Orders 100 (Lieber Code) Article 38.*

My entitlement is *"full acquittance and discharge for all purposes of the obligation of the person making the same (THE JOHN DOE STRAWMAN NAME ESTATE TRUST); and no person (no NAME ESTATE TRUST) shall be held liable in any court for or in respect to anything done or omitted in good faith in connection with the administration of, or in pursuance of and in reliance on, this section, or any rule, regulation, instruction, or direction issued hereunder" via full and complete INDEMNITY per General Orders 100, Article 38, and full reliance on title 12 USC 95(a)2.*

Therefore . . .

> 1. I have USED my *MONEY ORDER PROMISES TO PAY* in pursuance of and reliance on title 12 USC 95(a)2.
>
> 2. I have USED my *RECEIPT* (*my Birth Certificate Bond*) and the *NAME* stated thereon in pursuance of and reliance on title 12 USC 95(a)2.

3. EVERYTHING I do and have done in the past in behalf of this *NAME ESTATE* I do and have done in pursuance of and reliance on title 12 USC 95(a)2.

NOW therefore, *Mr. Public Official Administrator Trustee,* you need to do *YOUR* job and *acquit and discharge* the CLAIMS being made against this *defendant NAME ESTATE* in pursuance of and reliance on title 12 USC 95(a)2.

*All Rights Reserved*

/s/\_\_\_\_\_**John Smithton Doe**\_\_\_\_\_

John Smithton Doe (c) LS, Authorized Representative/Attorney-In-Fact for:
JOHN SMITHTON DOE
c/o Address
Zip City, State
nickname@emailaddress.net

*Subscribed To And Sworn To Before God [Titus 1:2] this XX.day of Month 20XX*

*Acknowledgement By Publication*

## AFFIDAVIT
## THE NAME OF THE GAME

STATENAME STATE     )
                    ) ss.
CountyName County   )

COMES NOW **John Smithton: Doe**, the natural living flesh and blood man, a peaceful American National on the land, under oath, who states that the following information is of his own personal knowledge, and belief.

The Income tax and all statutory law is imposed on the basis of the ***property rights*** of the corporate UNITED STATES in the USA and the corporate CROWN in Canada.

The same scheme can be found operating in any other subject country of the Pontiff of Rome's Holy Roman Empire. Thus, in actuality, the assumed ***property right*** is that of the Holy Roman Empire since the corporate CROWN and the corporate UNITED STATES are agencies of and for the Holy Roman Empire.

The CROWN is the administrative corporation of the Pontiff of Rome owned City of London, the financial, legal and professional standards capitol of and for the Vatican. The City of London, like Washington, D.C., is a square mile area within Greater London, England, which, like Washington, D.C., is an independent city-state.

In the USA, the administrative corporation for the Pontiff of Rome is the UNITED STATES corporation called Columbia, or the "District of Columbia", which administers Vatican capitol for military purposes. The UNITED

STATES also administers the 50 sub-corporate States of the United States of America, identified with the two-cap letters: – CA, OR, WA, ME, etc.

All human adults are deceived into using the fiction name that is imprinted on the copy of the birth certificate you receive when ordering it from State Vital Statistics, or from whatever source you apply to. Although the birth certificate is of a somewhat recent origin and used to formally offer **citizens** as **chattel in bankruptcy** to the Pope's Holy Roman Empire owned Rothschild Banking System, the false use of the family name goes back to the Middle Ages in England.

Thus, with the family name made a primary surname (example; Mister Jones), and the given name of the child (example; Peter) makes a reference name to the primary name; a reverse or mirror image to reality. A **family name** (surname) is NOT a man's name – it is a name of a Clan – of a blood relationship.

We are now **forced** or **obliged** to use that name in all commercial and Government dealings and communications. So when we *do* use it, as 99.99% of the human inhabitants of North America and most of the world do, we supposedly **voluntarily** attach ourselves, the free will adult human, to the Crown/State owned and created property called the **legal identity name** as an **accessory** attached to property owned by another party.

Think of a ship being towed by another ship. Which ship captain decides what route both ships will take? The **legal name/strawman** is the intermediate tow-rope, and the towing ship is the corporate (make-believe) ship at sea, the City of London Crown. As an attachment to the legal name owned by the Crown, you are the towed ship, and *your* vessel's captain, *your free will mind,* is a subservient crewmember to the captain of the Crown.

The State or Crown does not give us authority, nor grant, license, permission, or leave, to use the Crown or State owned **legal identity name**. Thus our use of the State owned **legal identity name** as an adult free will man [male or female] is a **form of theft** against a maritime jurisdiction entity [all incorporated bodies are **make-believe ships at sea**]. Under maritime law, the accused is guilty until proven innocent. This allows **the Roman Law system** which we have here in the United States, to impose **involuntary servitude** upon an adult woman or man. Involuntary servitude simply means **a slave stripped of granted rights** or a slave called a **citizen**; **subject**; a **free-man**.

These stripped rights include **due process of law** – no jury trial, and charges when no harm has been done against another man or his property with criminal intent.

We see this Roman Law in the US 13th Amendment II involuntary servitude instituted in the mid 1860's: **"Neither slavery nor involuntary servitude, except as a punishment for crime whereof the party shall have been duly convicted."**

The crime with which you have been convicted is the **unauthorized use of the Crown's or the State's intellectual property – the 'legal identity name'.**

The Crown/State then invokes the legal maxim, **accessio cedit principali** [*an accessory attached to a principal becomes the property of the owner of the principal*], where the principal is the **legal identity**

**name** as **intellectual property**. The owner is the corporation called the Crown/State, or UNITED STATES, and the accessory is **the free will human** who has supposedly volunteered himself to be **property under attachment** to the Crown/State.

A human adult who is property is of **slave status** - be it a **citizen, subject, or** a **free-man**.

The precept, that the relationship between **free will men** and Government/corporate bodies is contractual, is not correct. All **supposed** remedies in contract law, American UCC, or Canadian PPSA, are **red herring diversions** – some intended, and some in ignorance by teachers who see dollar $igns in teaching this, since it sounds authentic to those who don't realize that their Government sees them as slaves without the right to find remedy in statutory law.

As a slave, one's property in possession, including his body and labor, belongs to the slave owner 100%. And the slave owner's property right is a bundle of rights – to own, to use, to sell, to gift, to bequeath, and to hypothecate his property.

Thus, ALL **income** resulting from the owned human slave's mental and/or physical labor belongs to the slave owner. That which is left with or granted to the slave for his maintenance and use is called a **benefit**. In Canada, the **return of income** [*the phrase itself tells the story*] is called a **T1 tax and benefits package**. The **T1,** or **IRS 1040 (USA)** is an **accounting by the slave** of his fruits of labor that belong to the slave owner, **and the prescribed 'benefits' that he may keep or have returned back from withholding**.

Thus in reality, all income tax cases result from the

fraud, illegal concealment, and theft **of the slave owner's property** by the accused slave.

Going back to an above paragraph, we find that the attachment of oneself to the Crown/State owned name is **assumed to be voluntary** as the Crown/State corporations have no valid right to impose slavery upon human adults against their will, except as stated in the next paragraph.

Anyone working as an employee is in a contract of **voluntary servitude** = obedience and loyalty to — and direction and time control by — the employer. Until we who are **assumed to be slaves** get our heads around this **key to the lock** that holds our chains of slavery around our ankles and necks, we will continue to attempt to swim with that **100 lb. ball and chain** attached to our leg.

Another factor of the use of the **Roman Law system** is contained in the 1860's 13th Amendment to the US Constitution, the Constitution of the corporate UNITED STATES [not the 13th Amendment of the US Republic, circa 1819].

The latter 13th amendment says: **"Neither slavery nor involuntary servitude, except as a punishment for crime whereof the party shall have been duly convicted, shall exist within the United States, or any place subject to their jurisdiction."** Notice that this applies **only** to the corporate body called UNITED STATES INC.

All corporate bodies are **make-believe ships at sea** and are thus, **internally under maritime law** [*incorrectly called **admiralty law** unless applied to the military*]. In maritime law **the accused is guilty unless**

***proven innocent.*** Thus, a free-will adult man who uses the property of a corporate body **without its authority and consent** is under maritime jurisdiction. This makes a free-will man who uses a **corporate Crown- or corporate State-owned legal identity name** a **convicted criminal,** subject to the imposition of slavery, which is involuntary servitude.

You, as a child, were Crown or State property by way of the birth registry, and thus, you could use Crown or State property, meaning the all caps **legal identity name**. But when you became an adult, as a vessel on the sea of life, **as a sovereign captain/free will mind**, you no longer had a right to use that Crown or State owned **legal identity name** as an identity name.

Under the **property right** of slave ownership, in regard to property in the possession of an owned slave, a simple **demand** for the property by the slave owner, or his agent such as the IRS, or a county tax collector, or for a court imposed fine, is all that is necessary, without due process of law. Remember, *all* that a slave possesses belongs to the slave owner.

We are NOT saying here that you ARE a slave. It's just that the Government and its employees, judges, and officers, SEE you as a SLAVE.

A bill can only be paid with money; and there is no money, since the early 1930s. All that is left is some form of "promissory note".

Now, if you get a mortgage or a loan from a bank, instead of the bank lending you the money you created by your signed promissory note (the credit), they use it as payment for Notes or Computer values they create out of nothing in a computer, or for printing paper notes, but not the printed value on the note. You still create the value for the loan by your bill of exchange promissory note.

Further, when any **officer** of the corporate body chooses to declare someone **homo sacer** (*a man who has been stripped of his status as "person"; an obedient corporate slave member of the body politic*), he is stripped of the right of due process of law and can be fined, punished, tortured, or even killed, without repercussion to the office or officer involved. This happens all the time in the world of the Holy Roman Empire.

This doctrine of **homo sacer** is clearly presented in the **US Fugitive Slave Act of 1850**, Article 6:

> ***"In no trial or hearing under this act shall the testimony of such alleged fugitive be admitted in evidence; and the certificates in this and the first section mentioned, shall be conclusive of the right of the person or persons in whose favor granted, to remove such fugitive to the State or Territory from which he escaped, and shall prevent all molestation of such person or persons by any process issued by any court, judge, magistrate, or other person whomsoever."***
> —*http://www.yale.edu/lawweb/avalon/fugitive.htm*

**Three Major Points:**

**1. The accused disobedient slave cannot enter evidence in his own defense.** Sound familiar? The German Holocaust Denial litigation courts declared that ***"truth is no defense"***. Judges constantly ignore offered defenses **by Government accused defendants**

especially in traffic and income tax issues. And this might be acceptable if the judge were to explain **why** he needs to do this, but almost 100% of the time no explanation is offered, and this is to hide the **homo sacer doctrine** and the fact that a slave is being tried for disobedience to the rules of the slave owner's property right.

**2. The "certificate" presented by the officer or agent of the property owner** (his declaration of ownership) **is sufficient for conviction of disobedience** – (*the slave is guilty, unless proven innocent by an officer of the UNITED STATES or the CROWN.*)

**3. No molestation** (*such as criminal or civil complaints*) **can be made by or on behalf of the accused or convicted disobedient slave.** Does anyone know of successful litigation against a police officer or judge who severely abused the unalienable rights of a man? Well, there *may* be a few in well publicized cases where the system seeks to hide **their despotic Roman scheme,** but such cases are rare.

We are not suggesting that the Fugitive Slave Act is still being used; it was likely rescinded at some earlier time; however, the provisions written within that act were directly out of the **Roman Law system** in dealing with disobedient slaves, and **Roman Law** is being imposed upon the free will adult people in America and Canada who have **Roman slavery imposed upon them.**

English common law is, in reality, **Roman Municipal Law**, a form of maritime law where there is frequent use of the **"notwithstanding clause"** of all ships at sea and **make-believe ships at sea – incorporated bodies** – (*The captain may deviate from the rules when* *he deems it necessary* **"for the good of the ship"**). Thus, by using that rule **English common law is frequently referred to as "judge made law".**

## THE REMEDY

Since we are **forced to** or are **obliged to** use the Crown/State owned **legal identity name** in all commercial and government dealings, services, and communications, we can make a **claim of right** under the **Rule of Private Necessity** – with the necessity being the **means to sustain and maintain our life,** as all food, shelter, clothing, means of travel, and that which answers our need for happiness, has to be obtained or used in the realm of commerce.

This counters the claim that we **voluntarily** attach ourselves to Crown/State property.

Again. The Private Necessity is that we cannot do anything relative to life, liberty, property, or due process of law, without using the Crown/State owned name; thusly we cannot sustain or maintain our lives without that fiction name.

The legal all-caps name is always the person charged with the crime. The Government's intent is to get you, the adult man, attached to (identified with) that accessory name. And you and your children have to **use** that legal name in all commerce under private necessity.

Only in court do you need to prove:

    1. That you are a separate party from the all caps named defendant.

2. That you only use the legal name (named as the defendant) under private necessity to sustain and maintain your life and that you are *not* voluntarily attached to it permanently as an accessory to Crown property.

3. That the copy of the birth certificate held by oneself has been surrendered to the Court; that you deny any fiduciary responsibility for that Crown property or the name thereon.

4. It all comes down to **Informed consent**. You do not have to consent to being identified as the name found on the birth certificate. **"I do not authorize you to identify me as being the 'legal identity name' on your documents. I do not consent to being identified by any name."**

The name *they* use on all their documents is the all-caps legal name.

By presenting the Certificate of Birth to them and asking them investigate, two questions will repel all attacks:

1. Who has the secured title to the legal name JOHN DOE?

2. What rights do I have in the legal name?

The answers to these two questions will prove that (1), the government (aka, the secured party) secured the rights in the legal name and therefore I (you) have no rights in the legal name, and (2), If I (you) have no **rights** in the legal name, then how can I (you) have any **obligations** related to the legal name?

The party that the law holds legally responsible for the financial and other obligations of the property (the legal name) is the secured party, which, in the case of the legal name, is the government that is legally responsible for the financial and other obligations of the legal name property.

Hence, there is no place for the system to go once this truth is on the table. Certainly the claims of the IRS can be easily defeated with this approach.

However, the judge may make the assumption that by your so-called **permanent** use of the legal identity name, you have become an *accessory* attached to that Crown/State owned name, and thus you are the property of the Crown by the legal maxim which arises out of the property right, **accessio cedit principali**.

Thus, to complete the above procedure, you must, by *asseveration* (*formal affidavit*) or notice, claim by **right of free will** that you use the Crown/State owned name in commerce under private necessity to maintain and sustain your life. As such, your *use* of the Crown/State owned name is *not* a voluntary act by yourself.

Also, you could send a letter to the Secretary of State of your state asking for the authority, date, means, and methods by which you, a free will man, became a slave owned and controlled by the corporate UNITED STATES. If they do not offer such proof, or if they do not respond to your request, your proof is their **acceptance by silence** of your assertion that you are not a slave who is owned by the Crown or the State.

*All Rights Reserved*

/s/_____**John Smithton Doe**_____

John Smithton Doe (c) LS, Authorized Representative/Attorney-In-Fact for:
JOHN SMITHTON DOE
c/o Address
Zip City, State
nickname@emailaddress.net

*Subscribed To And Sworn To Before God [Titus 1:2] this XX.day of Month 20XX*

Acknowledgement By Publication

## AFFIDAVIT
## THE CREDIT RIVER DECISION

STATENAME STATE    )
                                ) ss.
CountyName County  )

COMES NOW **John Smithton: Doe**, the natural living flesh and blood man, a peaceful American National on the land, under oath, who states that the following information is of his own personal knowledge, and belief.

Almost 50 years ago, in 1968, in Credit River Township, Minnesota, the finding commonly referred to as the **Credit River Decision** of the landmark court case, **First National Bank of Montgomery, Minnesota, vs. Jerome Daly**, held the **Federal Reserve Act** to be unconstitutional and void. This decision, which is legally sound, *declared in effect, that all private mortgages on real and personal property, and all U.S. and State bonds held by Federal Reserve National and State Banks are null and void.*

This amounts to the *emancipation* of all Americans from *personal, national and state debt, purportedly owed to the Federal Reserve Bank*. Every American owes it to himself, his country, *and to the people of the world,* to study and understand this decision, for upon this decision hangs the question of *freedom or slavery for the world*.

— — —

On May 8, 1964, Mr. Jerome Daly executed a Note and Mortgage to the First National Bank of Montgomery, Minnesota, which is a member of the Federal Reserve

Bank of Minneapolis. Both banks are privately owned and are a part of the non-federal Federal Reserve Banking System.

In the spring of 1967, Mr. Jerome Daly was in arrears $476.00 in the payments on this Mortgage and Note. The Note was secured by a Mortgage on real property in Spring Lake Township in Scott County, Minnesota. The Bank foreclosed by advertisement and bought the property at a Sheriff's Sale held on June 26, 1967. Mr. Jerome Daly made no further payments after June 26, 1967 and did not redeem within the 12 month period of time alloted by law after the Sheriff's Sale.

The bank brought an action to recover possession of the property to the Justice of the Peace Court at Savage, Minnesota. The first 2 Justices were disqualified by Affidavit of Prejudice; the first by Mr. Daly, the second by the bank, and a third judge refused to handle the case. It was then sent, pursuant to law, to Martin V. Mahoney, Justice of the Peace, Credit River Township, Scott County, Minnesota, who presided at a Jury trial on December 7, 1968.

The Jury found the Note and Mortgage to be void for failure to give any validity to the Sheriff's Sale. The Verdict was for Mr. Daly with costs in the amount of $75.00.

The acting President of the Bank, Mr. Lawrence V. Morgan, admitted that the Bank created the money and credit upon its books, by which it aquired or gave as consideration for the Note; that this was standard banking practice; that the credit first came into existence when they created it; that he knew of no United States Statute which gave them the right to do this, and that this is the universal practice of these banks.

Mr. Lawrence V. Morgan appeared at the trial on December 7, 1968 and was perceived to be candid, open, direct, experienced, and truthful. He testified to 20 years of experience with the Bank of America in Los Angeles, the Marquette National Bank of Minneapolis, and as the Planiff in this case. He seemed to be familiar with the operations of the Federal Reserve System.

The banker testified about the mortgage loan given to Mr. Jerome Daly, and then Mr. Jerome Daly cross examined the banker about the creating of money "out of thin air".

Mr. Jerome Daly asked the Bank President, **"If you were just opening up your bank and no one had yet made a deposit, and I came into your bank and wanted to take out a loan of $18,000.00, could you loan me that money?"**

When the Bank President said, **"Yes"**, Mr. Jerome Daly then asked, **"Does this mean that you can create money out of thin air?"** And the Bank President said, **"Yes, we can create money out of thin air."**

He freely admitted that his Bank created all of the Money or Credit upon its books with which it acquired the Note and Mortgage of May 8, 1964. The credit first came into existence when the Bank created it upon its books by ledger entry. Further, he freely admitted that no United States Law gave the bank the authority to do this. There was obviously **no lawful consideration** for the Note. The Bank parted with **absolutely nothing** except paper and a bit of ink.

Justice Martin V. Mahoney then said, **"IT SOUNDS LIKE FRAUD TO ME"** and everbody in the court room nodded their heads indicating that they agreed with Jusice

Martin V. Mahney.

No complaint was made by the banker that the bank did not receive a fair trial. From the admissions made by Mr. Lawrence V. Morgan, the path of duty was clearly made and very direct and clear for the jury. Their verdict could not reasonably have been otherwise. Justice was rendered completely, and without denial, promptly, and without delay, freely, and without purchase, comfortable to the laws in this Court on December 7, 1968.

This was the first time the question has been passed upon in the United States. **This decision is one of the great documents of American history.** It is a huge cornerstone wrenched from the temple of Imperialism — **one of the solid foundation stones of Liberty.**

— — —

The **Credit River Decision**, as it is known, was and still is *the most important legal decision ever decided by a Trial Jury of 12 women and men!*

*All Rights Reserved*

/s/_____**John Smithton Doe**_____

John Smithton Doe (c) LS, Authorized Representative/Attorney-In-Fact for:
JOHN SMITHTON DOE
c/o Address
Zip City, State
nickname@emailaddress.net

*Subscribed To And Sworn To Before God [Titus 1:2] this XX.day of Month 20XX*

# AFFIDAVIT
## STAYING IN HONOR

STATENAME STATE     )
                              ) ss.
CountyName County   )

COMES NOW **John Smithton: Doe**, the natural living flesh and blood man, a peaceful American National on the land, under oath, who states that the following information is of his own personal knowledge, and belief.

The Founder's pledge in the last sentence of the Declaration of Independence of 1776 reads as follows:

> ***"And for the support of this Declaration, with a firm reliance on the protection of Divine Providence, We mutually pledge to each other our Lives, our fortunes, and our sacred Honor."***

So after pledging how does one **remain** in honor?

> ***"A victorious army appropriates all public money, seizes all public movable property until further direction by its government, and sequesters for its own benefit or of that of its government all the revenues of real property belonging to the hostile government or nation. The title to such real property remains in abeyance during military occupation, and until the conquest is made complete."*** — Part 31, of the Lieber Code.

Big deal; but what does this mean? Let's look at the keys words **appropriates, sequesters**, and **abeyance.**

***Appropriate:*** ...to take exclusive possession of...

***Sequester:*** ...to set apart; seize...

***Abeyance:*** ...temporary inactivity; in suspension...

So, now ***"substitute"*** those definitions and one can now see that *the victorious army takes exclusive possession of all titles while they are held in suspension and utilizes the revenues for its benefit until the conquest is complete.* How is the conquest completed? Could that be when *"peace"* has been declared?

> **"Private property, unless forfeited by crimes or by offenses of the owner, can be seized only by way of military necessity, for the support or other benefit of the Army or of the United States."** — Part 38, of the Lieber Code.

If the owner has not fled, the commanding officer will cause ***"receipts"*** to be given, which may serve the spoliated owner to obtain ***"indemnity"***.

You can call this part of the Lieber Code, the ***"usufruct clause"***. Why? Well, let's look up the term ***"usufruct"*** and its corresponding counterpart ***"usufructuary"***.

**Usufruct:** The right of enjoying a thing, the property of which is vested in another, and to draw from the same all the profit, utility and advantage which it may produce, provided that it be without altering the substance of the thing.

**Usufructuary:** ...one who has the right and enjoyment of an usufruct...

**DUTIES OF USUFRUCARY:**

> 1. To make an inventory of the things subject to the usufruct, in the presence of those having an interest in them.
>
> 2. To give security for their restitution; when the usufruct shall be at an end.
>
> 3. To take good care of the things subject to the usufruct.
>
> 4. To pay all taxes, and claims which arise while the thing is in his possession, as a ground rent.
>
> 5. To keep the thing in repair at his own expense.

So **Article 38** of **The Lieber Code** acknowledges that the **"occupational forces"** have a corresponding duty to *not alter the lands or the* **"producers of the fruit"** *upon which it needs to survive.* This is how the Romans were able to "conquer the world". They knew that if the lands were *"raped"* and *"torn asunder"* of the ability to produce what the army needed, the army was doomed. So, it would only take the *excess* for its needs and allow the lands and its *"inhabitants"* to keep what they needed to keep producing so the army would not starve, being so far away from **"Home"**.

Do not all roads lead to ***"Rome"***?

Now many of you who read this will begin to ask, *"Ok, this is all well and good for the (so-called) United States, but what about the rest of us?"*

Have no fear, the **"engineers"** of the **"system"** also thought of the rest of us, which why they had a little

Convention in a place called *"the Hague"* in 1907 and from that convention came Article 55, which states:

> *"The occupying State shall be regarded only as administrator and usufructuary of public buildings, real estate, forests, and agricultural estates belonging to the hostile State, and situated in the occupied country. It must safeguard the capital of these properties, and administer them in accordance with the rules of usufruct.*

It was nice of them to include the rest of the world within the confines of this *"war"*. But how are the rest of us *"included"*? Could it be that wherever the IMF [US Treasury; Fed Res] *"intervenes"* with a *"bailout"*; this *"system"* is then *"implemented"*?

Why else would *"they"* be in Iraq, Iran, Afghanistan, and Pakistan? I'll bet if you look at *"history"*, you will find that the IMF had *"loaned"* or *"given"* them some sort of *"assistance"*. Now, everyone can participate in the *"perfection"* that is *"the system"*.

You will also notice that all **Social Security** and **Birth Certificates** fall under the Dept of Commerce and Agriculture (*of agricultural estates*). Do you really think that this was by accident?

—— —— ——

Now, back to *"how does one stay (remain) in honor?"* They thought of that as well and to prevent undermining the *sacredness"* of that honor, the *"engineers"* placed within the nature of the system a method of *"testing the people"* for their *"intentions"* (*subconscious; hearts*). The general operation of such method is found with the book **"Military Government and Martial Law"**.

> *"The rule that certain of the enemy's subjects are to be treated as non-combatants gives rise to the correlative duty on their part to refrain from acts of hostility. This obligation is enforced with great rigor by the dominant power. Inhabitants of the country militarily occupied are not permitted to make war as they please; being soldiers one day and engaged in peaceful pursuits the next. In the instructions for United States Armies such persons are called war rebels."*

In other words, **you WILL be persecuted** because the **"first essential task"** as outlined in **"US Army Doctrine and Belligerent Occupation"** is to **"restore public order and safety"** as per the Hague Convention Article 43 which states.

> *"The authority of the legitimate power having in fact passed into the hands of the occupant, the latter shall take all measures in his power to restore, and ensure, as far as possible, public order and safety, while respecting, unless absolutely prevented, the laws in force in the country. This task is significant for three reasons. First, it allows the peaceful inhabitants of an occupied territory to continue with their day-to-day lives. Second, it allows the occupant and the local inhabitants to form an agreement to maximize their benefits to both. Third, this task is so broad that it encompasses many of the functions associated with government administration."*

Again: The first essential task is to **"restore public order and safety"**.

Now you can see what is happening.

Once you wish to become a **peaceful inhabitant** you must first declare your intent to engage in a **treaty of peace**. In doing so, you understand that the *occupational army/government* holds *ownership control* of all *titles* in **defense of the pledge** encapsulated within the last line of the Declaration of Independence. In order to **defend that sacred honor** the *peacekeeper* must **"surrender all claims of ownership"** to the occupying government.

To ensure that the *peacekeeper* remains in honor and stands firm, honoring the pledge, the *occupational government* must *put your feet to the fire* to ensure that *public order and safety* be implemented and ensured. And it carries out this *function* with *great rigor*.

The resulting *"treaty of peace"* allows the *peaceful inhabitant* to live day-to-day without interference while ensuring both parties (*the inhabitant and occupational government*) co-exist for each other's *mutual (equitable) benefit*. Once this is established, the **occupational government** then **exists** to carry out that agreement.

So basically, the **occu pational government** exists to ensure that peace is maintained and fulfilled. In doing so, it becomes a **usufructuary** with respect to you, provided that you honor the **sacred commitment**. If you do, that **government** will ensure that you are protected and have every opportunity to live your life to your fullest potential, but you must toss aside all your prejudices and have nothing but faith and trust that those duties will be carried out.

Now, we must warn you that, since there is a correlative duty to refrain from acts of hostility, once one decides to *"come to peace"* you also have an implied, unwritten duty **to PROTECT the integrity of the illusion** *(the system)* because it is *"that illusion"* which *"forces" man to grow up, develop his mind and abilities, and adapt to hardships enabling spiritual growth.*

If one should FAIL to *"PROTECT the illusion",* then no matter how *"right"* one is or how peaceful one appears, *"the system"* will REJECT you as a parasite or disease because now you threaten the *symbiosis* of the whole. In other words, just because you *know* the *system* is based upon an *illusion;* what makes you think you have the right to *destroy it* because parts of it *appears* to be *evil* or *disgusting* in your view?

Remember **"sacred honor"**? You must honor the WHOLE, not just the parts that suit your desires, needs or wants. **Ain't love grand?**

Possess nothing but love in your heart and being with the utmost desire for the best for everyone.

But first, you must *understand and know* **who the problem is.** And just maybe, you will *emulate the pledge* encapsulated within that last line of *the Declaration,* **and become the change you seek**.

*All Rights Reserved*

/s/_____**John Smithton Doe**_____

John Smithton Doe (c) LS, Authorized Representative/Attorney-In-Fact for:

JOHN SMITHTON DOE
c/o Address
Zip City, State
nickname@emailaddress.net

*Subscribed To And Sworn To Before God [Titus 1:2] this XX.day of Month 20XX*

*Acknowledgement By Publication*

# AFFIDAVIT
# REGARDING THE IRS

STATENAME STATE    )
                                 ) ss.
CountyName County    )

COMES NOW **John Smithton: Doe**, the natural living flesh and blood man, a peaceful American National on the land, under oath, who states that the following information is of his own personal knowledge, and belief.

The problem is that neither the "Internal Revenue Service" nor "INTERNAL REVENUE SERVICE" which are run under the auspices of the FEDERAL RESERVE, nor the "IRS" which is run under the auspices of the IMF, are government agencies, they are subcontractors hired as bill collectors by the "IRS", and as accountants by the INTERNAL REVENUE SERVICE.

It's hardly worth going after the lackeys. The ones responsible are much higher up the food chain.

The One Number used as both "your" Social Security Number and "your" Taxpayer Identification Number is used to keep track of two accounts—one records <u>credit due to you</u> and the other one records <u>debts due to the IRS</u>. The IRS (IMF) keeps track of the <u>debt side</u>, and the INTERNAL REVENUE SERVICE (FEDERAL RESERVE) keeps track of the <u>credit side</u>.

The IRS sends a bill to you in the name of "JOHN QUINCY ADAMS" — a STATE-owned ESTATE trust, for charges related to the government services provided by UNITED STATES INC. This is just business, howbeit, it involves known mail fraud. The so-called "tax" is a bill for public services rendered — Defense, roads, you name it.  And so far as that goes, it is a perfectly justifiable bill which is purposefully and self-interestedly misaddressed. The debt side of "your" account is run by the "IRS" under the familiar number **123-45-6789** *with dashes*. Dashes = debt side of the ledger.

Where this all falls apart is the *presumption* that the STATE franchise and UNITED STATES INC are making: that you, the living man, are responsible *for providing private credit* for this public debt, and that you have *"voluntarily"* agreed to act as an *unpaid federal employee known as a "withholding agent"*.  They never explained anything about their *"system"* to you, and certainly did not provide *"full disclosure"* so you are well within your rights to object and invoke your Common Law right preserved by UCC 1-308 and 1-103.6 *not to be bound by any defective contract,* including those that are unilateral, lacking full disclosure, which are inequitable, not in-kind, tainted by fraud, entered into by Third Parties merely claiming to "represent" you, or which are deemed to exist as a result of your receiving *any compelled benefit* or fruit of monopoly inducement (*bribe*).

You can *"just say no"* to the IRS and sever any further *presumption* or *relationship* with them as of the end of the  federal fiscal year (June 30) of any year you choose. You simply *invoke your rights* stated above and send the IRS a polite letter referencing 26 USC 6013 and telling them that you are **"revoking your election to pay"** as of the 30th of June.

However, as irritated as we all are, and as unjust and criminally misrepresented the administration of the *so-called "income tax"* has been, we also have to admit that government services have to be paid for.  So now we come to the *other side* of the account ledger. The *credit side* of "your" account is operated under *"your"* Social Security Number *without dashes and enclosed by asterisks*: **\*123456789\*** by the "INTERNAL REVENUE SERVICE" run by the FEDERAL RESERVE that has recently reorganized under the auspices of the UNITED NATIONS INC.

Technically, you have never owed any "income" tax, ever, in your life. The very word "income" is a corporate accounting term. Corporations accrue "income". Living people accrue "property". That's the legal definition long and short of it.

What has been done by those claiming to "represent" you, is to set up various legal fiction entities operated under your given name. So the debts of "JOHN QUINCY ADAMS" are the debts of a federally owned and operated ESTATE Trust located in Puerto Rico, and as a legal fiction entity— a corporate entity— it does accrue "income". In fact, because the rats have unlawfully and without your knowing consent "converted" your bank account to the ownership of this ESTATE Trust, every dime that you "donate" to "JOHN" is considered taxable income.

This is how the IRS prosecutes its victims— it claims that you owe the debts of this Puerto Rican ESTATE Trust and uses the confusion caused by the semantic deceit of "similar names" to entrap you into their court proceedings and then use the already accomplished unlawful conversion of your bank account to seize funds held in the NAME of "JOHN QUINCY ADAMS".

All this nastiness could be avoided, if this system were functioning properly, and the debts of "JOHN QUINCY ADAMS" were being paid by the Internal Revenue

Service — which is what should be happening. The Internal Revenue Service now being operated as the INTERNAL REVENUE SERVICE has control of the credit side of the "JOHN QUINCY ADAMS" account, and there is plenty of credit in his account to discharge any debt that "HE" owes, however, since the IRS is billing you, instead of billing "HIM", you get caught in the crossfire quite unnecessarily.

The Secretary of the Treasury has without justification "blocked" most of these *credit accounts* and pretends that the beneficiaries of these ESTATES are "unknown"— even though they manage to find you readily enough when they are trying to collect a debt, they pretend that you are "missing" when it comes time to pay you. Most recently the rats have attempted to redefine your ESTATE Trust which is operated under your name styled like this: "JOHN QUINCY ADAMS" and run by the Washington, DC. Municipal Government, as a "transmitting utility" owned and operated by the United Nations City State and doing business under your name styled as in: "JOHN Q. ADAMS".

Please note that "JOHN Q. ADAMS" is not even a legal and specific and clearly identifiable name— it could be relate to a man named John Quincy Adams or another man named John Quentin Adams, and so on.

These semantic deceits resulting in false claims and identity theft and misappropriation of credit and mis-administration of the public trusts are the heart of the real fraud practiced and fostered by the "Internal Revenue Service" / "IRS" system.

We — especially the judges and law enforcement and military men and politicians — have got to put a stop to this craziness and mis-administration and identity theft, or there will be nothing stopping any foreign state and any private corporation from creating legal fiction entities "in our names" and bringing false charges against us.

As for this history–

The 1933 amended issue of the 1917 Trading With the Enemy Act falsely declared that the American People - the Employers of the United States of America - are "enemies" and conscripted, that is "borrowed" both us and our property "for the war effort". Now it should be recognized that no corporation has the right to declare "war" on anyone or anything, and that the men doing this had no granted authority to "represent" us in any such manner or fashion, much less authority to lay a false claim against the employers of the United States of America, Inc. It was fraud then and it is fraud now. All claims based upon it are null and void and the officials merely need to be called on it and held feet first to the flames.

However, they did this—as they did their take over of the monetary system via the "Federal Reserve Act"— another piece of fraud—under conditions of secrecy and semantic deceit. In this way the banks running the "Federal Reserve System" placed a false claim of ownership against our assets and us— our land, our businesses, our homes, everything.

After the First World War ended, they failed to return our property to us. They kept it. And in 1933 gratuitously included us and all our property as part of their bankruptcy. They falsely claimed that we were standing as "voluntary sureties" for the debts of the now-bankrupt "United States of America, Inc." and its "State of State" franchises.

So, having "borrowed" our assets, they now falsely claimed that we were responsible for their debts, and in this manner, enslaved and obligated us, just as a co-signer on a car loan is obligated. Again, none of this was fully disclosed, and the nature of the "United States of America, Inc." as merely a privately owned and operated governmental services corporation being run by the Federal Reserve banks was never revealed to the American People.

As a result of these acts of fraud and false pretenses Americans have labored for over a hundred years to pay debts that they largely never owed and have been grossly imposed upon and defrauded by people they trusted who owed them the fiduciary trust that they violated.

As of July 1, 2013, Pope Francis cleaned house and settled the "bankruptcy" of the United States of America, Inc. At that point, all the Puerto Rican ESTATE trusts should have been formally dissolved, and all assets presumed to belong to them should have been returned to their true beneficiaries, the living American people. Instead, the criminals in DC contrived to work out another "New Deal" with the operators of the United Nations City State.

The United Nations City State has allowed the old criminals who were running the "Federal Reserve System" to reorganize as the "new" "FEDERAL RESERVE" under UN auspices. This criminal syndicate has claimed — falsely as ever— that all the property contained in the individual ESTATES was "abandoned" and therefore belongs to the banks, and they have begun to transfer all title and ownership of OUR property and assets into their brand new transmitting utilities doing business under the "JOHN Q. ADAMS" names.

Pope Francis gave them three years to come into compliance with their corporate charters or face being liquidated. More than the three years has passed, and thus far, they are laughing in his face and doing everything they can to rob, rape, pillage, damage, and confuse the American People they have victimized for so long.

Make no mistake — these people running both the FEDERAL RESERVE and the IMF are criminals and these organizations are international criminal syndicates which have enslaved and falsely indebted the American People via identity theft, the practice of personage, unlawful conversion of assets, fiduciary trust fraud, kidnapping, inland piracy, contract default increasing the public debt, and myriad other offenses.

The American People are owed all their assets back, together with the interest and profit which have been made off those assets. The American organic States are *similarly* owed all their assets back. All that was "borrowed" must be returned, and any false pretense that UNITED STATES INC or any "successor" to this fraud—the UNITED NATIONS INC, for example — has no right to continue controlling Americans or their property via this network of fraud, and all false claims must cease.

This is what the officials have done to Americans and America. Every one of them who knew the truth and did nothing about it, are criminals in our midst. Now that it is becoming known, it is only a matter of time before the similar frauds that have impacted Europe and the former Commonwealth will become self-evident and the perpetrators forced out of their holes like the criminals they are and prosecuted as such on both a national and international basis.

Let that end come and come quickly. Let the sorting of the goats from the sheep begin. Those who have been complicit through ignorance must come out of Babylon, or be destroyed within it.

*All Rights Reserved*

/s/_____**John Smithton Doe**_____

John Smithton Doe (c) LS, Authorized Representative/Attorney-In-Fact for:
JOHN SMITHTON DOE
c/o Address
Zip City, State
nickname@emailaddress.net

*Subscribed To And Sworn To Before God [Titus 1:2] this XX.day of Month 20XX*

*Acknowledgement By Publication*

# AFFIDAVIT
## REDEMPTION DEMAND

STATENAME STATE    )
                               ) ss.
CountyName County  )

COMES NOW **John Smithton: Doe**, the natural living flesh and blood man, a peaceful American National on the land, under oath, who states that the following information is of his own personal knowledge, and belief.

**THAT** the Affiant has recinded the presumptive pledge of his assets that the federal UNITED STATES has hypothecated without his knowledge and consent and re-hypothecated as security and collateral for the Public Debt that it borrowed at interest from the non-federal Federal Reserve Bank. Affiant is hereby taking back, via redemption, credit that the corporate UNITED STATES took from him.

**THAT** the Federal Reserve Notes used in commerce today as instruments of Public Debt are primary debt obligations of the corporate UNITED STATES to the American people, and secondary debt obligations of the UNITED STATES to the private non-federal Federal Reserve Bank, and that "Private property shall not be taken for public use without just compensation." (Article VI of the Bill of Rights).

**THAT** the Affiant rebuts the presumption that his assets have lawfully been subrogated to the UNITED STATES which has taken them by presumptive pledge, and rebuts the claim that such subrogation makes Affiant liable for the obligations of the corporate UNITED STATES to the private non-federal Federal Reserve Bank.

**THAT** the Affiant hereby discharges all negative charges of debt with his positive charge of credit tendered in lawful promissory notes which govern in commerce as money substitutes today until lawful "money of account of the United States" is restored.

**THAT** the Affiant hereby exercises the REMEDY that Congress has given to him for equity interest recovery on his credit risk. Congress has extended to Affiant (an unincorporated, flesh and blood, living person) the right to issue and tender promissory notes for equity interest recovery toward repayment of the National Debt.

**THAT** Public Policy HJR-192 of 1933 gives the Secured Party Creditors of the corporate UNITED STATES the right to issue and tender private promissory notes "upon the full faith and credit of the United States" as evidences of the debt of the federal UNITED STATES to the private non-federal Federal Reserve Bank.

**THAT** no creditor can require tender of any specific type of currency such as gold or silver coin in place of promissory notes tendered in good faith for unlawful debt. (paraphrased from HJR-192 of 1933).

**THAT** the REMEDY for equity-interest recovery via *mutual offset credit exemption exchange* is codified in statutory law although virtually unknown and seldom utilized by people in commerce today.

*All Rights Reserved*

/s/_____**John Smithton Doe**_____

John Smithton Doe (c) LS, Authorized Representative/Attorney-In-Fact for:

JOHN SMITHTON DOE
c/o Address
Zip City, State
nickname@emailaddress.net

*Subscribed To And Sworn To Before God [Titus 1:2] this XX.day of Month 20XX*

*Acknowledgement By Publication*

# AFFIDAVIT
## NOTE TO MONEY ORDER PAYEE

STATENAME STATE    )
                               ) ss.
CountyName County  )

COMES NOW **John Smithton: Doe**, the natural living flesh and blood man, a peaceful American National on the land, under oath, who states that the following information is of his own personal knowledge, and belief.

**THAT** when making a loan, banks routinely monetize the customer's promissory note by making a book entry in an internal checking account secretly established in the customer's name, and saying to the customer *"You now have a new deposit with us."*

**THAT** as a Secured Party Creditor of UNITED STATES, INC, I am authorized by Congress to create money with my signature. (HJR 192, Public Law 73-10, of 1933)

**THAT** as a Secured Party Creditor of UNITED STATES, INC, I generate credit by the energy of my labor backed by the future commercial energy that I produce, so all of my debts are prepaid. (HJR 192, Public Law 73-10, of 1933)

**THAT** the Federal Reserve Bank of New York says in its publication, *"I Bet You Thought"* that *"Money does not have to be issued by a government or be in any special form."*

**THAT** Article IX of the Bill of Rights says that:*"The enumeration in the Constitution of certain rights shall* *not be construed to deny or disparage others retained by the people."*

**THAT** under the authority of Article IX of the Bill of Rights, the right to issue bills of credit and to declare the same to be legal tender for the payment of public and private debts has been by the people retained.

**THAT** under the laws of equity, the corporate UNITED STATES cannot hypothecate and re-hypothecate the private property and wealth of its private citizens and put them at risk as collateral for its fiat currency and debt obligations to the Federal Reserve Bank without providing them with an equitable REMEDY for recovery of interest on their risk that is due and payable to them upon demand.

**THAT** UNITED STATES INC does not violate the law by using the people's property as collateral for loans and to back is fiat paper money substitutes because it provides the sovereign citizens of America with a lawful REMEDY for the recovery of what is due them as accrued interest on its use and risk of their assets and wealth so that UNITED STATES INC can legally hypothecate and re-hypothecate the private assets and wealth of the people of the United States to the FEDERAL RESERVE BANK to back its fiat currency and debt obligations, with the people's credit, material substance, and implied consent.

**THAT** the authority for this REMEDY is found in Public Insurance Policy Bond HJR-192 of 1933, Public Law 73-10.

**THAT** all fiat currency of UNITED STATES INC since 1933, represents prepaid CREDIT backed by the real property, wealth, assets, and future labor of the sovereign people of America that UNITED STATES INC took by presumptive pledge and re-pledged as a primary obligation to the sovereign people of America and a secondary obligation to the non-federal FEDERAL RESERVE BANK.

**THAT** the attorneys who devise the public laws and regulations that Congress rubber-stamps which administer the ongoing bankruptcy reorganization of UNITED STATES INC, anticipated the long term destructive effect of its inflationary debt-based monetary system that many in government fear, so they made the statutory provisions for REMEDY to provide equity-interest recovery and repayment to their Sureties, sovereign Americans, and at the same time repayment on the National Debt.

**THAT** since the real property, wealth, and assets of all Americans is the faith and substance that backs the obligations, fiat currency, and debt obligations of UNITED STATES INC such credit has been tacitly offered and can be expressly accepted and utilized for equity-interest recovery via *mutual offset credit exemption exchange.*

**THAT** Public Insurance Policy Bond HJR-192 of 1933 provides for the discharge of every debt obligation of the federal UNITED STATES INC and its municipal subdivisions by pre-paying dollar for dollar the debt obligations owed to UNITED STATES INC against the same dollar for dollar amounts that the UNITED STATES INC owes to us, by thusly providing this REMEDY for equity-interest recovery and the payoff of the national public debt.

**THAT** "The public debt is that portion of the total federal debt that is held by the public." (31 USC 1230).

**THAT** Public Policy HJR-192 of 1933 and 31 USC 5103 gives private unincorporated people (the Secured Party Creditors of the federal United States) the right to issue legal tender promissory notes "upon the full faith and credit of the United States" as its obligations to them.

**THAT** this REMEDY for the recovery of equity-interest via *mutual offset credit exemption exchange* is codified in statutory law, even though this REMEDY is seldom utilized by the people in commerce today because it is virtually unknown.

**THAT** Federal Reserve Notes are promissory extension notes of debt that Congress has promised to redeem for us with offsets of prepaid credit upon our demand.

**THAT** a bill is a demand for payment in real "money of account of the United States" that cannot be made because there is no real "money of account of the United States" in use today with which to pay such demands. Federal Reserve Notes *discharge* debt whereas the sovereigns private personal credit *pays* debt; *extinguishing it completely*.

**THAT** our private personal credit (our promise to pay) pays debt when we accept a bill for its value with our promissory note endorsement and return its value to the sender to offset, zero, and balance the sender's account.

**THAT** HJR-192 of 1933 did not order the people to use Federal Reserve Notes to discharge debt. It simply *allows* them to use FRN's if they so choose, instead of *mutual offset credit exemption exchange.*

**THAT** people use Federal Reserve Notes *voluntarily* whether they know it or not.

**THAT** since there is no real "money of account of the United States" a monetary charge (a bill) is an invitation for you to settle the debt with Federal Reserve Notes or with *mutual offset credit exemption exchange.*

**THAT** a debtor has the option of *discharging* his debts with Federal Reserve Notes or *paying* his debts with his HJR-192 right of *mutual offset credit exemption exchange.*

*All Rights Reserved*

/s/_____**John Smithton Doe**_____

John Smithton Doe (c) LS, Authorized Representative/Attorney-In-Fact for:
JOHN SMITHTON DOE
c/o Address
Zip City, State
nickname@emailaddress.net

*Subscribed To And Sworn To Before God [Titus 1:2] this XX.day of Month 20XX*

*Acknowledgement By Publication*

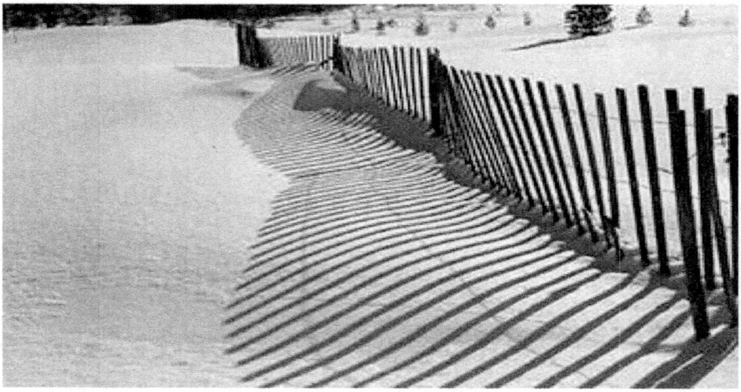

# AFFIDAVIT
## I AM NOT THE NAME

STATENAME STATE    )
                                ) ss.
CountyName County   )

COMES NOW **John Smithton: Doe**, the natural living flesh and blood man, a peaceful American National on the land, under oath, who states that the following information is of his own personal knowledge, and belief.

I, who shall not be with LEGAL name, hereby proclaim to all with unclean hands;

Be it now known that all words/spellings upon/within this document shall be of my will and intent only, without assumption/presumption on/of/by/for any/all concerned where my free will choice shall never be trespassed where my intent is my intent and no one else's;

WHEREAS, a great fraud has been revealed and is laid bare where unclean hands are now in the light exposed for all to see where any/all with unclean hands must judge only self, toto genere;

WHEREAS, non-disclosure has intent to defraud in that act, any and all contracts of body, mind, and soul are null and void, nunc pro tunc, praeterea, praeterea, praeterea ab initio, ad infinitum in this willful intent to commit fraud by omission and/or commission where others and all are concerned, and;

WHEREAS, threat of force perceived or real is proof of intent inasmuch as aiding and abetting in this fraud and where assumption and presumption are concerned and thus destroyed, whereby one is known by their actions of their willful intent either knowingly or in ignorance of the Divine laws under which all stand, and;

WHEREAS, all signatures, contracts, assumptions, presumptions etc et al are rendered null and void ab initio inasmuch as all are in contempt and fraud where the CROWN owned and COPYRIGHTED name DAVID EVERETT ROBINSON is concerned, and;

WHEREAS, the intent to commit fraud via deceptions/deceptios and willful non-disclosure of truths where intent to enslave all humanity/mankind by church/state in this intent is exposed fully whereby one's actions make one known, and;

WHEREAS, all names registered are, in fact, property of the CROWN/VATICAN, all matters pertaining to such names registered and the use thereof render all parties fraudulent and in contempt via willful intent to deceive and/or ignorance of use where all matters of church/state remain matters of church/state where use of the name/s registered are concerned and where/when third party interloping is evident by my use or anyone's use of stated registered names, and;

WHEREAS, it is not my intent to commit fraud or any *contemptible/contempt able* acts, it is also my equal intent to never aid and abet any other living soul via willfully knowing or ignorance on/in their/my part and any use of or claim made using the aforementioned name/s will render such attempt an act of fraud by willful commission, and;

WHEREAS, any/all use of church/state identification based upon these/all CROWN COPYRIGHTED name/s or any variation/s thereof renders the user in fraud absolute via their ignorance and by omission of disclosure of/by church/state, and;

WHEREAS, any/all claims made by any/all parties/agents/living souls upon another willfully or in ignorance to do so is guilty of fraud in that action by commission and/or omission of bearing false witness and is in contempt of church/state/self and is willfully aiding and abetting fraudulent deception/deceptios whereupon judgment is rendered upon any/all agents of church/state/self by the very action of claiming via CROWN COPYRIGHT fraud, and;

INASMUCH as intent (spirit) must be proven where all are concerned, it is now incumbent upon the church/state that the willful intent to commit fraud ab initio is without intent to do so. With prior knowledge, the agents/clergy/BAR members/all bound by oaths etc. et al to/of/for/by/with church/state did/do willfully deceive humanity and is, by the actions of all bound to church/state by oaths sworn/taken/given judged by/of/in all acts of harm upon any/all harmed, and;

WHEREAS, fraudulent intent of all bound to church/state entities/Identities/living souls/principalities is visible via omission and/or commission by the actions of harm/intent to harm of/for/by all beings using a NAME in fraud ab initio, all claims made/coerced/assumed/presumed etc. et al are in fact fraudulent at source of/for/by all claiming any/all legal NAME(S)/fictional identities/titles etc. et al and/or thus any/all forms/aliases and are of/by/for the criminal intent to do so using the intellectual property of another living soul/spirit or dead fictional entity where I am toto genere, spirit, mind, body, and;

FURTHERMORE, to engage in such intently destructive acts of harm/deception/theft/coercion etc. et al against another via any/all means is shown by one's actions and need never be judged whereby the act is the judge in/of itself, judge not lest ye be judged where assumption/presumption cannot/does not/will not exist after the act itself, and;

FURTHERMORE, any/all REGISTRATION/REGISTERING/REGISTER by omission and/or commission where full disclosure is not evident, the intent of church/state/any/all claiming such association/joinder by means of willful oaths, signatures (cursive), titles, etc. et al are, in fact, willful acts of predetermined fraud knowingly or unknowingly where wrongful obligation(s)/curse(s) has/is/was the intent where obligation(s) is/are replaced back upon those who knowingly and/or in ignorance of their fraud do so ab initio, ad infinitum, nunc pro tunc, praeterea, praeterea, praeterea, and;

FURTHERMORE, it is/was never my intent to willfully use the property of another WHEREAS, any/all things REGISTERED are, in fact, claimed to be such intellectual property of another, namely church/state/CROWN where my Mother and Father (deceased), unknowingly were, in ignorance, aided and abetted of their consent into such church/state contracts, be they all forms physical/spiritual/mental, and;

FURTHERMORE, I place the onus (ownus) back upon/return to any/all beings by virtue of their oaths etc. et al and self-judged in their acts, any/all obligations created by any/all contracts where all contracts entered into based on this fraud/original sin/intent to defraud are nullified/null and void ab initio, ad infinitum nunc pro tunc, and;

FURTHERMORE, all obligations upon myself created

via this fraud are void inasmuch as the perceived/assumed/presumed gift, without consideration of any all NAME(S) is concerned in that a BOND/DEBT was/is/has been created in the form of a BIRTH CERTIFICATE with an assigned DEBT, not value, where I was assumed/presumed to be that value without/void of my willful consent where it was/is/has been the willful intent of/by/for all parties initiating such acts of obligation upon this, their DEBT, and;

WHEREAS, intent is clearly visible by any/all who engage in acts of commerce (Whore of Babylon) using the NAME (mark of the beast) is/was/has been/will be acting in fraud and creating harm/cannibalism against their fellow humans/beings since all fiat currency is based upon aforementioned BONDS and is guilty of human being trafficking of the highest order and in defiance of creation where consumption ensues, and;

WHEREAS, the willful intent from any/all willful associates/members/oathed beings of church/state/CROWN is evidentiary proof of/by/for any/all acts perpetrated against another where any/all REGISTERED NAMES are concerned inasmuch as nondisclosure by aforementioned was never given/offered where aiding and abetting in fraud is the intent and where any/all aforementioned have unclean hands accordingly, and;

WHEREAS, any/all REGISTERED "things/possessions" are, in fact, property of the church/court/state/CROWN (copyright) where any claim made by any/all not oathed to the aforementioned are matters of church/court/state/CROWN inasmuch as willful trespass and enticement into slavery via third party interloping into such matters that do not concern me, the one who shall not be of NAME where my own customary calling is mine and shall never be given, and;

FURTHERMORE, by means of this BIRTH CERTIFICATE (long form/short form) deception/nondisclosure/willful act of fraud, the only DOCUMENT(S) ever willfully given as proof of intent to commit fraud/aid and abet fraud by/of/for church/court/state/CROWN etc. et al and all oathed/bonded to willfully to such titles/fictions/corporations where the claim is also made that the aforementioned take on the role of perceived parens patriea (embodiment of state) and have/are, in fact, kidnapped/abused/harmed any/all who have been fraudulently claimed to be a "ward of admiralty" where the Mother is fiduciary, Father is beneficiary ab initio and; WHEREAS, the rites of both Mother/Father have been stolen via nondisclosure and willful intent as proofed by actions of those, by oath/willful appli cation(s) any/all claiming to be of/for/by church/court/state/CROWN in the form of BIRTH CERTIFICATE(S)/license's/marriages/FAMILY NAME(S)/taxes/registrations etc. et al ab initio therefore;

Is it the/your willful intent of this/you of/for/by/in church/court/state/CROWN etc. et al beings living/dead fictions to coerce, by force or deceptive means, to have me incriminate myself where I am in full knowledge of this dual fraud where willful intent to do so makes me/you guilty ab initio by claiming to own/be something that is/was/has never been mine/yours to be/claimed?;

Is it your (by oath entity) intent to aid and abet the furtherance of this fraud/cannibalism/child kidnapping/human trafficking/theft etc. et al via fictitious ACTS/LEGISLATION etc. et al by/of/for dead entities by/for/of dead entities (dead carrying out the dead) where I am one of the living versus a fictional dead entity created by/for/of the church/court/state/CROWN by enticing me via force/coercion/deception to be a surety for the church/state/court/CROWN created debt(s)?;

WHEREAS, any/all fraud by virtue of its intent and creation remains as such, regardless of length of time taken for such any/all frauds to be exposed, all contracts are null and void upon its discovery where a fraud revealed is, in fact, null and void, ab initio, nunc pro tunc where all energies stolen in any/all forms shall be returned where the intent to commit fraud against me has been/is/will be with INTENT;

It is not/has never been/never will be my intent to willfully and knowingly commit fraud where mistakes in ignorance by commission and/or omission are present and where any/all acts of mine are not in contempt(with temptation) of anyone/anything where any being choosing willfully to contempt me is now with intent to do so. All contracts/documents/signatures/agreements etc. et al are now null and void where any/all DEBT created by church/state/court/CROWN is forgiven/returned from whence it was created (forgive us our debts as we forgive our debtors) where I am the noncontracting living with the debt BOND identity that is the property/responsibility (re-spawns-ability) of that/those which created it;

It is FURTHERMORE the obligation of any/all oathed beings of/by/for the church/state/court/CROWN to return my energy/creations/life-force stolen via this original sin/intent to defraud my Mother and Father where they aided and abetted in my own fraud by means of deception/nondisclosure where your unclean hands are/have been concerned. I seek no vengeance, I offer no judgments and return the obligations of debts/forgiveness to those who would/have deceived me where a crime against all humanity has been/is being perpetrated with willful intent in the light for all to see;

By one's actions one is known and instantly judged

in/of/for/by such actions where the intent is laid bare for all to see in/of/by/for any/all such actions WHEREAS, all/any beings willfully by/for/of commission/omission are held and bound judged of themselves. Act accordingly, lest ye be judged in/of/for/by oneself/yourself fully toto genere.

*All Rights Reserved*

/s/_____**John Smithton Doe**_____

John Smithton Doe (c) LS, Authorized Representative/Attorney-In-Fact for:
JOHN SMITHTON DOE
c/o Address
Zip City, State
nickname@emailaddress.net

*Subscribed To And Sworn To Before God [Titus 1:2] this XX.day of Month 20XX*

*Acknowledgement By Publication*

# AFFIDAVIT
## BANKER'S TESTIMONY

STATENAME STATE )
) ss.
CountyName County )

COMES NOW **John Smithton: Doe**, the natural living flesh and blood man, a peaceful American National on the land, under oath, who states that the following information is of his own personal knowledge, and belief.

We've all heard the saying: BANKS "create" MONEY out of NOTHING. Right? Not true! Read this fascinating revelation.

Testimony of a banker

The banker was placed on the witness stand and sworn in. The plaintiff's (the borrower's) attorney asked the banker the routine questions concerning the banker's education and background.

The attorney asked the banker, "*What is court exhibit A?*"

The banker responded by saying, "*This is a promissory note.*"

The attorney then asked, "*Is there an agreement between Mr. Smith (the borrower) and the defendant?*"

The banker said, "*Yes.*"

The attorney asked, "*Do you believe the agreement includes a lender and a borrower?*"

The banker responded by saying, *"Yes, I am the lender and Mr. Smith is the borrower."*

The attorney asked, *"What do you believe the agreement is?"*

The banker quickly responded, saying, *"We have the borrower sign the note and we give the borrower a check."*

The attorney asked, *"Does this agreement show the words 'borrower', 'lender', 'loan', 'interest', 'credit', or 'money' within the agreement?"*

The banker responded by saying, *"Sure it does."*

The attorney asked, *"According to your knowledge, who was to loan what to whom according to the written agreement?"*

The banker responded by saying, *"The lender loaned the borrower a $200,000 check. The borrower got the money and the house and has not repaid the money."*

The attorney noted that the banker never said that the bank received the promissory note as a loan from the borrower to the bank. She asked, *"Do you believe an ordinary person can use ordinary terms and understand this written agreement?"*

The banker said, *"Yes."*

The attorney asked, *"Do you believe you or your company legally own the promissory note and have the right to enforce payment from the borrower?"*

The banker said, *"Absolutely we own it and legally*

have the right to collect the money."

The attorney asked, "Does the $200,000 note have actual cash value of $200,000? Actual cash value means the promissory note can be sold for $200,000 cash in the ordinary course of business."

The banker said, "Yes."

The attorney asked, "According to your understanding of the alleged agreement, how much actual cash value must the bank loan to the borrower in order for the bank to legally fulfill the agreement and legally own the promissory note?"

The banker said, "$200,000."

The attorney asked, "According to your belief, if the borrower signs the promissory note and the bank refuses to loan the borrower $200,000 actual cash value, would the bank or borrower own the promissory note?"

The banker said, "_The borrower would own it if the bank did not loan the money_. The bank gave the borrower a check and that is how the borrower financed the purchase of the house."

The attorney asked, "Do you believe that the borrower agreed to provide the bank with $200,000 of actual cash value which was used to fund the $200,000 bank loan check back to the same borrower, and then agreed to pay the bank back $200,000 plus interest?"

The banker said, "No. If the borrower provided the $200,000 to fund the check, there was no money loaned by the bank so the bank could not charge interest on money it never loaned."

The attorney asked, *"If this happened, in your opinion would the bank legally own the promissory note and be able to force Mr. Smith to pay the bank interest and principal payments?"*

The banker said, *"I am not a lawyer so I cannot answer legal questions."*

The attorney asked, *"Is it bank policy that when a borrower receives a $200,000 bank loan, the bank receives $200,000 actual cash value from the borrower, that this gives value to a $200,000 bank loan check, and this check is returned to the borrower as a bank loan which the borrower must repay?"*

The banker said, *"I do not know the bookkeeping entries."*

The attorney said, *"I am asking you if this is the policy."*

The banker responded, *"I do not recall."*

The attorney again asked, *"Do you believe the agreement between Mr. Smith and the bank is that Mr. Smith provides the bank with actual cash value of $200,000 which is used to fund a $200,000 bank loan check back to himself which he is then required to repay plus interest back to the same bank?"*

The banker said, *"I am not a lawyer."*

The attorney said, *"Did you not say earlier that an ordinary person can use ordinary terms and understand this written agreement?"*

The banker said, *"Yes."*

The attorney handed the bank loan agreement marked "Exhibit B" to the banker. She said, *"Is there anything in this agreement showing the borrower had knowledge or showing where the borrower gave the bank authorization or permission for the bank to receive $200,000 actual cash value from him and to use this to fund the $200,000 bank loan check which obligates him to give the bank back $200,000 plus interest?"*

The banker said, *"No."*

The lawyer asked, *"If the borrower provided the bank with actual cash value of $200,000 which the bank used to fund the $200,000 check and returned the check back to the alleged borrower as a bank loan check, in your opinion, did the bank loan $200,000 to the borrower?"*

The banker said, *"No."*

The attorney asked, *"If a bank customer provides actual cash value of $200,000 to the bank and the bank returns $200,000 actual cash value back to the same customer, <u>is this a swap or exchange</u> of $200,000 for $200,000."*

The banker replied, *"Yes."*

The attorney asked, *"Did the agreement call for an exchange of $200,000 swapped for $200,000, or did it call for a $200,000 loan?"*

The banker said, *"A $200,000 loan."*

The attorney asked, *"Is the bank to follow the Federal Reserve Bank policies and procedures when banks grant loans."*

The banker said, "*Yes.*"

The attorney asked, "*What are the standard bank bookkeeping entries for granting loans according to the Federal Reserve Bank policies and procedures?*" The attorney handed the banker FED publication "Modern Money Mechanics", marked "Exhibit C".

The banker said, "*The <u>promissory note</u> is recorded as a <u>bank asset</u> and a new <u>matching deposit</u> (liability) is created. Then we issue <u>a check from the new deposit</u> back to the borrower.*"

The attorney asked, "*Is this not a <u>swap or exchange</u> of $200,000 for $200,000?*"

The banker said, "*This is the standard way to do it.*" The attorney said, "*Answer the question. Is it a swap or exchange of $200,000 actual cash value for $200,000 actual cash value? If the note funded the check, must they not both have equal value?*"

<u>The banker then pled the Fifth Amendment</u>.

The attorney asked, "*If the bank's deposits (liabilities) increase, do the bank's assets increase by an asset that has actual cash value?*"

The banker said, "*Yes.*"

The attorney asked, "*Is there any exception?*"

The banker said, "*Not that I know of.*"

The attorney asked, "*If the bank records a new deposit and records an asset on the bank's books having actual cash value, would the actual cash value always* come from a customer of the bank or an investor or a lender to the bank?"

The banker thought for a moment and said, "*Yes.*"

The attorney asked, "*Is it the bank policy to record the promissory note as a bank asset offset by a new liability?*"

The banker said, "*Yes.*"

The attorney said, "*Does the promissory note have actual cash value equal to the amount of the bank loan check?*"

The banker said "*Yes.*"

The attorney asked, "*Does this bookkeeping entry prove that <u>the borrower provided actual cash value</u> to fund the bank loan check?*"

The banker said, "*Yes, the bank president told us to do it this way.*"

The attorney asked, "*How much actual cash value did the bank loan <u>to obtain the promissory note</u>?*"

The banker said, "*Nothing.*"

The attorney asked, "*How much <u>actual cash value</u> did the bank receive from the borrower?*"

The banker said, "*$200,000.*"

The attorney said, "*Is it true <u>you received $200,000 actual cash value from the borrower,</u> plus monthly payments and then you foreclosed and never invested one cent of legal tender or other depositors' money <u>to obtain the promissory note in the first place</u>? Is it true that <u>the borrower financed the whole transaction</u>?"

The banker said, *"Yes."*

The attorney asked, *"Are you telling me <u>the borrower agreed to give the bank $200,000 actual cash value for free</u> and that the banker returned the actual cash value back to the same person as a bank loan?"*

The banker said, *"I was not there when the borrower agreed to the loan."*

The attorney asked, *"Do the standard FED publications show <u>the bank receives actual cash value from the borrower for free</u> and that the bank returns it back to the borrower as a bank loan?"*

The banker said, *"Yes."*

The attorney said, *"Do you believe the bank does this without the borrower's knowledge or written permission or authorization?"*

The banker said, *"No."*

The attorney asked, *"To the best of your knowledge, is there written permission or authorization for the bank to transfer $200,000 of actual cash value from the borrower to the bank and for the bank to keep it for free?"*

The banker said, *"No."*

The attorney said, *"Does this allow the bank to use this $200,000 actual cash value to fund the $200,000 bank loan check back to the same borrower, forcing the borrower to pay the bank $200,000 plus interest?"

The banker said, "*Yes.*"

The attorney said, "*If the bank <u>transferred $200,000 actual cash value from the borrower to the bank</u>, in this part of the transaction, did the bank loan anything of value to the borrower?*"

The banker said, "*No.*" He knew that someone must first deposit something having actual cash value (cash, check, or <u>promissory note</u>) to fund a check.

The attorney asked, "*Is it the bank'policy to <u>first transfer the actual cash value from the alleged borrower to the lender</u> for the amount of the alleged loan?*"

The banker said, "Yes."

The attorney asked, "*Does the bank pay IRS tax on <u>the actual cash value transferred from the alleged borrower</u> to the bank?*"

The banker answered, "*No, because the <u>actual cash value transferred shows up like a loan from the borrower</u> to the bank, or a <u>deposit</u> which is the same thing, so it is not taxable.*"

The attorney asked, "*If a loan is forgiven, is it taxable?*"

The banker agreed by saying, "*Yes.*"

The attorney asked, "*Is it the bank policy <u>to not return the actual cash value that they received from the alleged borrower unless it is returned as a loan</u> from the bank to the alleged borrower?"

The banker replied *"Yes."*

The attorney said, *"You never pay taxes on the <u>actual cash value you receive from the alleged borrower and keep</u> as the bank property?"*

*"No. No tax is paid"*, said the crying banker.

The attorney asked, *"When the lender receives the actual cash value from the alleged borrower, <u>does the bank claim that it then owns it and that it is the property of the lender</u>, without the bank loaning or risking one cent of legal tender or other depositors' money?"*

The banker said, *"Yes."*

The attorney asked, *"Are you telling me the bank policy is that the bank owns the <u>promissory note</u> (<u>actual cash value</u>) without loaning one cent of other depositors' money or legal tender, that the alleged borrower is the one who provided the funds deposited to fund the bank loan check, and that the bank gets funds from the alleged borrower for free?"*

*"Is the money then returned back to the same person as a loan which the alleged borrower repays when the bank never gave up any money to obtain the promissory note?*

*"Am I hearing this right? I give you the equivalent of $200,000, you return the funds back to me, and I have to repay you $200,000 plus interest? Do you think I am stupid?"*

In a shaking voice the banker cried, saying, *"<u>All the</u>*

*banks are doing this. Congress allows this.*"

The attorney quickly responded, "*Does Congress allow the banks to breach written agreements, use false and misleading advertising, act without written permission, authorization, and without the alleged borrower's knowledge to transfer actual cash value from the alleged borrower to the bank and then return it back as a loan?*"

The banker said, "*But the borrower got a check and the house.*"

The attorney said, "*Is it true that the actual cash value that was used to fund the bank loan check came directly from the borrower and that the bank received the funds from the alleged borrower for free?*"

"*It is true*", said the banker.

The attorney asked, "*Is it the bank policy to transfer actual cash value from the alleged borrower to the bank and then to keep the funds as the bank's property, which they loan out as bank loans?*"

The banker, showing a wince of regret that he had been caught, confessed, "*Yes.*"

The attorney asked, "*Was it the bank's intent to receive actual cash value from the borrower and return the value of the funds back to the borrower as a loan?*"

The banker said, "*Yes.*" He knew he had to say yes because of the bank policy.

The attorney asked, "*Do you believe that it was the borrower's intent to fund his own bank loan check?*"

The banker answered, *"I was not there at the time and I cannot know what went through the borrower's mind."*

The attorney asked, *"If a lender loaned a borrower $10,000 and the borrower refused to repay the money, do you believe the lender is damaged?"*

The banker thought. If he said no, it would imply that the borrower does not have to repay. If he said yes, it would imply that the borrower is damaged for the loan to the bank which the bank never repaid. The banker answered, *"If a loan is not repaid, the lender is damaged."*

The attorney asked, *"Is it the bank policy to take actual cash value from the borrower, use it to fund the bank loan check, and never return the actual cash value to the borrower?"*

The banker said, *"The bank returns the funds."*

The attorney asked, *"Was the actual cash value the bank received from the alleged borrower returned as a return of the money the bank took or was it returned as a bank loan to the borrower?"*

The banker said, *"As a loan."*

The attorney asked, *"How did the bank get the borrower's money for free?"*

The banker said, *"<u>That is how it works</u>."*

*. . . And so it is!*

*"You don't get a mathematically Perfected Economy*

*from snake oil salesmen; you get division."*

Source

*Modern Money Mechanics, A Workbook on Bank Reserves and Deposit Expansion,* by the Federal Reserve Bank of Chicago (see Page 6, Paragraph 6)

*"What they do when the banks/money changers make alleged loans is to accept promissory notes or the alleged borrower's promissory note in exchange for credits to the alleged borrower's transaction account). Alleged loans/assets and deposits/liabilities both rise by the amount of the alleged loan."*

CONCLUSION:

The only consideration the bank risks is the mere cost of publication, which is the mere cost to publish a further representation, (bank money or credit), that evidences the former issuance of one of our <u>promissory obligations</u> or <u>notes</u>, which would, then, amount to <u>about $2</u> to publish <u>the $200,000 that the alleged borrower</u> *creates by his signature on a promissory note,* <u>before the bank's book entry</u>.

The "bankers/money changers" give up no consideration equal to the debt they falsify to themselves. The local bank uses the *alleged borrowers credit worthiness* meaning the *lawful consideration given by him via his promissory note,* and then,

Borrow money from a central bank who in turn then publishes a further representation, which is a purposed misrepresentation of the former contractual obligation, or misrepresentation of the obligors issuance of a promissory note so as to then allegedly loan a further representation or a misrepresentation, (bank money, credit) to the alleged borrower.

The $2 dollars the bank may give up is redeemed in a fraction of the first loan repayment by the alleged borrower.

<u>The interest the central bank charges to the local bank</u>, (using the obligor's or alleged borrowers consideration to publish the bank money), <u>is always lower than what the local bank charges</u> on an alleged loan <u>to the alleged borrower</u>, thus, the <u>difference in interest rates is the local banks unearned profit</u> (unjust reward) <u>for stealing & laundering</u> (principal & interest) <u>into the hands of the central bank system</u>.

Both the central bank & the local banks risk nothing of their own, the local banks always use "the alleged borrowers promissory notes as their consideration (not the bank's consideration), to borrow money that we the people create upon conception of the note.

No new money comes into existence until someone issues a <u>promissory obligation</u> first. The bank money did not exist <u>until an alleged borrower walks into the bank & signs a promissory note FIRST</u>.

*All Rights Reserved*

/s/_____**John Smithton Doe**_____

John Smithton Doe (c) LS, Authorized Representative/Attorney-In-Fact for:
JOHN SMITHTON DOE
c/o Address
Zip City, State
nickname@emailaddress.net

*Subscribed To And Sworn To Before God [Titus 1:2]
this XX.day of Month 20XX*

*Acknowledgement By Publication*

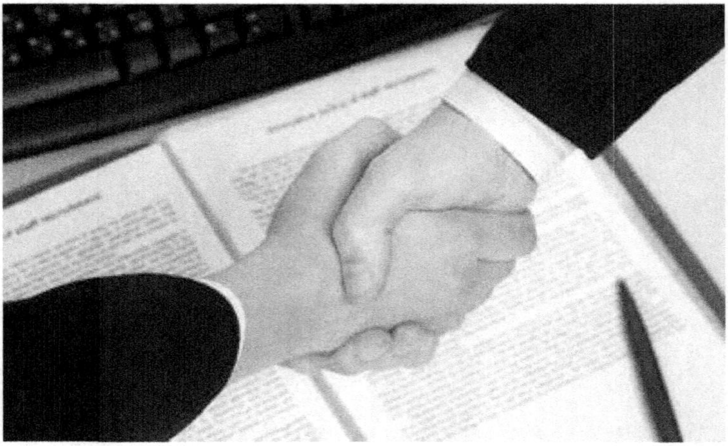

# AFFIDAVIT
## AFFIDAVIT OF TRUTH

STATENAME STATE      )
                     ) ss.
CountyName County    )

COMES NOW **John Smithton: Doe**, the natural living flesh and blood man, a peaceful American National on the land, under oath, who states that the following information is of his own personal knowledge, and belief.

> ***"Indeed, no more than an affidavit is necessary to make the prima facie case."***
> *(United States v. Kis, 658 F.2nd, 526, 536 (7th Cir. 1981); Cert. Denied, 50 U.S. L.W.2169; S. Ct. March 22, 1982).*

**THAT** the Affiant is a flesh and blood man, and is sovereign in a collective capacity with other sovereigns

**THAT** the Affiant's rights *"existed by the law of the land long antecedent to the organization of the State."* *(Hale. v. Henkel, 201 U.S. 43)*

**THAT** the Affiant's rights exist even in light of the U.S. Bankruptcy *aka* The National Emergency, and that includes the right of redemption.

**THAT** under Article I, Section I of the Maine Constitution, *"The people have all power"* and the Affiant as one of the people can exercise any power.

**THAT** the Affiant is *"one of the people"* and is above the corporate government called the "State of Maine"/ STATE OF MAINE, operating in a de-facto bankrupt capacity/status.

**THAT** the Affiant filed a UCC Financing Statement (UCC-1) in Maine State, UCC Filing Number 2040001673309-45 on 06/09/2004 to perfect a security interest to initiate commercial redemption as a matter of right.

**THAT** the Affiant is the Secured Party creditor and authorized representative of the corporate fiction-entity/Debtor (*Ens legis*) identified as DAVID EVERETT ROBINSON; under necessity.

**THAT** the Affiant caused to be filed a Superior Security Interest and Lien upon the property of the Debtor; and in the Debtor's name filed first in line and first in time over and above the State of Maine, and that all property is exempt from levy.

**THAT** the State of Maine cannot show nor provide a superior interest in the said property as identified upon the private Security Agreement held by the Affiant. (*see for reference; Wynhammer v. People, NY 378*).

**THAT** the Affiant/Secured Party is flesh and blood, and the corporate fiction/Debtor/Ens legis, as appearing on any UCC filing, is "artificial" and was created in the contemplation of law (commerce) AND THE TWO ARE NOT THE SAME, FOR ONE IS REAL, THE OTHER IS FICTION.

**THAT** any discrimination or injury caused by any failure of the State of Maine to recognize the two entites as distict, the one real and the other artificial, agrees to such injuries and associated damages as established by the Affiant and the State, by and through its agents, by said agreement and is estopped from defense or rebuttal in the matter and agrees that the Affiant may proceed for damages by Tort.

**THAT** this Affidavit if not rebutted point for point by any man, representing the State of Maine at any level, in any matter, at any time within 7 days upon receipt, these facts stand in both the private and public record... as true.

**NOTE**: Maxim of Law; 1) In Commerce Truth is sovereign. 2) For a matter to be resolved, it must be expressed. Point of Law: Silence equates to agreement.

*All Rights Reserved*

/s/_____**John Smithton Doe**_____

John Smithton Doe (c) LS, Authorized Representative/Attorney-In-Fact for:
JOHN SMITHTON DOE
c/o Address
Zip City, State
nickname@emailaddress.net

*Subscribed To And Sworn To Before God [Titus 1:2] this XX.day of Month 20XX*

*Acknowledgement By Publication*

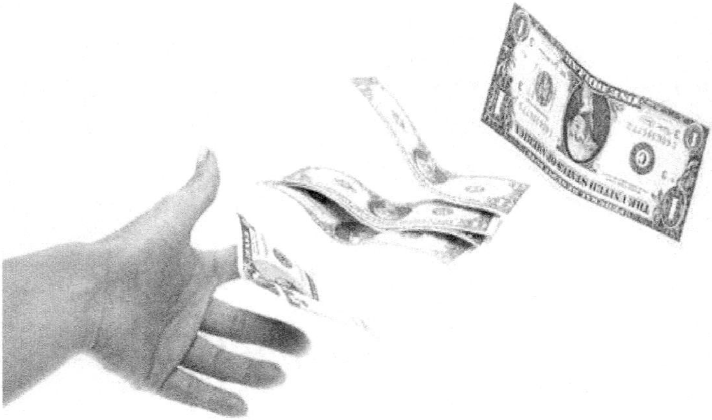

AFFIDAVIT
**ADMINISTRATIVE NOTICE**

STATENAME STATE      )
                                      ) ss.
CountyName County    )

COMES NOW **John Smithton: Doe**, the natural living flesh and blood man, a peaceful American National on the land, under oath, who states that the following information is of his own personal knowledge, and belief.

    **THAT** under the laws of equity, the UNITED STATES cannot hypothecate and re-hypothicate the private property and wealth of its private citizens and put them at risk as collateral for its fiat currency and credit obligations to the Federal Reserve Bank without providing the private citizens of America with a lawful equitable REMEDY for recovery of interest on their risk, that is due and payable to them upon demand.

    **THAT** the UNITED STATES does not violate the law because the UNITED STATES provides the sovereign citizens of America with a legal REMEDY for the recovery of what is due them as accrued interest on the use and risk of their assets and wealth so that it can legally hypothecate and re-hypothecate the private wealth and assets of the people to the Federal Reserve Bank to back its fiat currency and debt obligations with their material substance, credit and implied consent.

    **THAT** the provisions for this REMEDY are found in Public [Insurance] Policy HJR-192 of 1933, i.e. Public Law 73-10.

    **THAT** all UNITED STATES fiat currency since 1933

represents CREDIT backed by the real property, wealth, assets and future labor of the sovereign people of America that the UNITED STATES has taken by presumptive pledge and re-pledged as a secondary obligation to the non-federal Federal Reserve Bank.

**THAT** the attorneys who devise the public laws and regulations which Congress rubber-stamps that orchestrate the bankruptcy reorganization of the corporate UNITED STATES anticipated the long term inflationary effect of its debt based monetary system that many in government feared so they made statutory provisions for this REMEDY to provide equity-interest, recovery-payment to their Sureties (sovereign Americans), and at the same time payments on National Debt.

**THAT** since the real property, wealth and assets of all Americans is the faith and substance that backs the obligations, fiat currency and credit of the UNITED STATES, such credit has been tacitly offered to the people and can be accepted and used for equity-interest recovery via mutual offset credit exemption exchange.

**THAT** Public Policy HJR-192 of 1933 provides for the discharge of every debt obligation of the federal UNITED STATES and its sub-divisions by discharging dollar for dollar the obligations that are owed them offset against the same dollar for dollar amounts that the UNITED STATES owes us, thus providing this REMEDY for equity-interest recovery and the eventual payoff of the public (national) debt.

**THAT** *"the public debt is that portion of the total federal debt that is held by the public."* (31 USC 1230).

**THAT** Public Policy HJR-192 of 1933 and 31 USC 5103 gives private unincorporated people (the Secured Party Creditors of the federal UNITED STATES) the right to issue legal tender promissory notes "upon the full faith and credit of the UNITED STATES" as obligations of the federal UNITED STATES to them.

**THAT** this REMEDY for the recovery of equity-interest via mutual offset credit exemption exchange is codified in statutory law although this benefit is virtually unknown by the people and therefore seldom utilized in commerce today.

**THAT** Federal Reserve Notes are promissory notes of debt that Congress has promised to redeem for us with offsets of credit upon our demand.

**THAT** a bill is a demand for payment in real "money of account of the United States" that cannot be made because there is no real "money of account of the United States" in use today with which to pay one. Federal Reserve Notes "discharge" and our personal credit "pays" debt instead.

**THAT** our personal credit (our promise to pay) pays debt when we accept a bill for its value with our *promissory note endorsement* and return its value to the sender to offset, zero and balance the sender's account.

**THAT** using Federal Reserve Notes is optional whether we know it or not.

**THAT** HJR-192 of 1933 did not "order" people to use Federal Reserve Notes to discharge debts, it simply "allows" them to use FRNs if they choose to do so.

**THAT** people use Federal Reserve Notes voluntarily whether they know it or not.

**THAT** since there is no real "money of account of the United States", a monetary charge is an offer to contract to settle the debt with either Federal Reserve Notes or with a mutual offset credit exemption exchange.

**THAT** a debtor has the option of *"discharging"* his debts with Federal Reserve Notes, — or *"paying"* his debts with his mutual offset credit exemption exchange.

*All Rights Reserved*

/s/_____**John Smithton Doe**_____

John Smithton Doe (c) LS, Authorized Representative/Attorney-In-Fact for:
JOHN SMITHTON DOE
c/o Address
Zip City, State
nickname@emailaddress.net

*Subscribed To And Sworn To Before God [Titus 1:2] this XX.day of Month 20XX*

*Acknowledgement By Publication*

AFFIDAVIT
**ACCEPTANCE FOR VALUE**

STATENAME STATE      )
                     ) ss.
CountyName County    )

COMES NOW **John Smithton: Doe**, the natural living flesh and blood man, a peaceful American National on the land, under oath, who states that the following information is of his own personal knowledge, and belief.

## BACKGROUND

The Europeans who came to North America were 'grubstaked' by others (probably the East India Trading Company and the Bank of England). It was a huge venture which required large amounts of money to get it started. So the 'colonists' got their start based on hard money loans…back in the days of hard money.

Once the colonists were established, they incorporated in order to deal with the burden of their debt. The first incorporation was under the Articles of Confederation. The effect of the Articles was two-fold: first to protect the interests of the creditors, and secondly to protect the assets of the colonists who were working to establish a new economy.

The Articles of Confederation were weak in dealing with international contracts and the enforcement of Admiralty/Maritime concerns. So the Articles were rolled into what was then called the Constitution for the united States of America which tied up the loose ends left by the Articles.

Since the people were trying to stave off bankruptcy liquidation and preserve the fruits of their labors the Constitution operated in bankruptcy re-organization mode, and so since it was operating in bankruptcy, the law form of the national government had to be Admiralty.

Bankruptcy re-organization exists in Admiralty. Bankruptcy liquidation exists in Common Law. Common law is always repugnant to the federal or national government. The states used the common law and liquidation.

So there was that distinction between the bankruptcies operated in the national versus the state governments.

Then a glitch came along with the Constitution regarding the minting of money. The national government decided to stop using gold for money, and stopped minting it, and passed a law demanding that all **US citizens** turn in their gold, and once the gold was safely confiscated, they passed a law making it illegal for **US citizens** to own gold.

This caused a dilemma in commerce. If there was no money, how could the people conduct commerce?

Well for the answer, the government looked to the Law Merchant law form for a substitute for money. Instead of using gold for money, the government adopted the policy that citizens would use what the merchants considered "good as gold", that is, notes of credit and bills of exchange, called Negotiable Instruments.

The Law Merchants had successfully used bills of exchange and notes of credit for centuries with complete success, so their way of commerce and accounting in trade and was adopted for use by the united States, which adopted the use of bills of exchange and notes of credit under the Negotiable Instruments Act of the 1800's.  This eventually evolved into the Uniform Commercial Code, rules and regulations for commerce regarding bills and notes instead of silver and gold.

With this new form of "money" came a new form of accounting — double-entry bookkeeping — balancing credits and debits to reach equity: a zero balance.

The zero balance is paramount in double-entry bookkeeping which has become a stumbling block for many who do not understand that this is the system of accounting we are operating under today.  Double-entry bookkeeping determines if equity and fairness exist. If the bookkeeping indicates inequity, we have to stop and make an adjustment to restore fairness.

This change in law form and type of money used in commerce began in 1933, when the Federal Reserve Act of 1913 became international law, under the law of proscription, since it had not been objected to during the twenty years since then. With the Federal Reserve Act, government and commerce were changed from a gold metal standard to a promise note standard — from substance money of exchange to fictional money of account.

Once the government began to operate its fictions, certain new considerations had to be met.  The first steps that had to be taken had to do with sureties and bonds.

In Admiralty, everything works as insurance, a future indemnity against injury or loss. We have to give assurance to those around us that we will not harm them by what we do. This can be in the form of a bond. A bond is a future indemnity against injury. And together with a bond, we must provide a way to collect against the bond in the form of some surety backing the bond.

So the people of the united States were pledged into an association for the mutual benefit of all concerned. The pledge that one member would not require another member to pay association debt. In other words, the tacit pledge to forgive association members their debts as they forgive *their* debts, consideration of contracts in the form of *forgiveness of debts* one to another.

This *forgiveness of debt* results in taxable events because *before giveness* is not *giveness.*

A debt must be paid or discharged in order to have justice. But that is *not* to say that the debt cannot be prepaid! An anticipated debt can be paid before the debt is incurred, instead of being dealt with after the fact. It became public policy in 1933 that the remedy for US citizens regarding public debt is that *all subsequent debt is prepaid.*

The problem was that the government never explained this to its citizens, but kept it hidden from the people in a controlled way. The people were kept in the dark about how this "New Deal" really worked, hence the people have been robbed by many of those who *do* understand.

When we pay for something before it is required it can only be deemed a prepay. So when we forgive, the *forgive part* was contemplated prior to the *give,* hence remedy is created, before it is required.

When the government decided to go to double-entry bookkeeping and money of account rather than substance and money of exchange, bonds and sureties had to be put up to protect the creditors of the bankruptcy. So this bond is best embodied in HJR 192 of June 5, 1933, elsewhere codified as Statute 73-10. This congressional Act is the *indemnity* provided for any future liability.

HJR 192 is the *guarantee* that all public debts are prepaid. HJR 192 is the actual PAYMENT itself, IN FACT.

Now, one would naturally want to find out what the surety for that bond would be. What is the guarantee of HJR 192? It must be found in the substance that creates the shadow. The surety can't be found in the shadow or in the fiction. The surety is the people; the property created by their labor. The evidence that surety has been pledged for the guarantee of the bond is the birth certificate.

Here the people are insuring themselves by their labor to guarantee that their bookkeeping is correct. The people are the creditors of all public business and property.

All substance produced in the public domain must eventually be returned (*from the public domain*) to the people (*the original creditors*).

The "money" we are using in the public domain is money of account, which is the agreement that all the participants in the association will abide by the Lord's Prayer, **"forgive us this day our debts, as we forgive others their debts..."** The debts were anticipated and the remedy was created prior to the debt.

Commercially, it might be put something like this: **"Apply HJR 192 to our debts, as we apply it to the debts of others."** It's the same process indeed.

— — —

So, how do we make some sense of this *"accepted for value"* process that seems to be so popular today? How does it apply?

Since the people guarantee the liability in the public domain by accepting the benefit of limited liability to the public debt, the people are the creditors of the national bankruptcy. The people are the SPONSORS OF THE CREDIT - via their promises.

The United States has been operating Chapter 11 bankruptcy re-organization. The one who filed for the bankruptcy is called the "debtor in possession" (*the one who is in debt*). If any creditor dishonors the bankruptcy, the debtor in possession (as the trustee) will liquidate the creditor — dollar for dollar — the dishonor amount, — because he has become delinquent. The creditor was obligated to settle the debt, when asked to do so, but refused.

Any request made by the debtor to the creditor MUST BE ACCEPTED and given credit value. If not, the creditor becomes delinquent and gets liquidated by the debtor. So, if a debtor comes to the creditor and says, **"forgive me this day my debts"** and the creditor does not openly and freely forgive the debtor his debt, the Lord will call him to account for dishonoring the pledge of the prepayment of debts.

In theology it is called blasphemy against the Son of God; in commerce, it is called a violation of public policy.

It would be dishonoring the benefit that has already been pledged when the person became a part of the association and guaranteed that he would not hold each other accountable for any public liability or debt.

So let's look at the public liabilities we are required to forgive. A public liability is anything that can be shown as an entry on a double-entry bookkeeping account. If it can't be entered in double-entry accounting it is most likely a private matter; not in the public realm.

You can easily discern a public versus a private communication. The public request for adjustment will always come directly to the trust account — the title of which is styled in *all capital letters,* such as JOHN H. SMITH. This is a direct attempt to attach to the bond of the JOHN H. SMITH TRUST. It is a violation of public policy to attach to a future liability to avoid a present liability. Look at this diagram:

| Presentment | Promissory | Indemnity |
| BILL | NOTE | BOND |
| Past liability | Present liability | Future liability |

Here is a typical demonstration of how a greater debt is used to indemnify (insure) a smaller debt. The BILL represents a past liability, where the NOTE represents the present liability, and the BOND is the *indemnity* for a future liability not yet determined.

A secret scheme was devised to attach to the bond of the trust representing the labor of the men and women who have put themselves up as surety for the national debt. The attempt of the holder of a past obligation to bypass the present liability and go directly to the future bond.

Instead of settling the matter in the here and now, the attempt is made to enslave the surety in some future event by attaching the bond.

The way to prevent this is to take the BILL that's been directly sent to the BOND and bring it into the present **by accepting the bill and giving it value** and returning it to the presenter for settlement and closure of the account.

When that is done we have defeated the fraudulent scheme to put us in debt of future liabilities by attaching the bond.

*All Rights Reserved*

/s/_____**John Smithton Doe**_____

John Smithton Doe (c) LS, Authorized Representative/Attorney-In-Fact for:
JOHN SMITHTON DOE
c/o Address
Zip City, State
nickname@emailaddress.net

*Subscribed To And Sworn To Before God [Titus 1:2] this XX.day of Month 20XX*

*Acknowledgement By Publication*

AFFIDAVIT
# CRIME OF THE CENTURY

STATENAME STATE      )
                     ) ss.
CountyName County    )

COMES NOW **John Smithton: Doe**, the natural living flesh and blood man, a peaceful American National on the land, under oath, who states that the following information is of his own personal knowledge, and belief.

## The Crime Of The Century

When they're trying so hard to pull the wool over your eyes, maybe it's to hide something you should be trying extra hard to see...

NOTE: With only a couple of obvious exceptions, links in the following article are documentation proving the assertion being made. It is recommended that you click on all of them.

TWELVE YEARS AGO, CORRUPT ELEMENTS in the United States Department of Justice, Internal Revenue Service and federal judiciary began the commission of a grave crime directly affecting a few folks in Michigan, but aimed at all of America. Here's the story.

Three years earlier, in 2003, a book called 'Cracking the Code- The Fascinating Truth About taxation In America' (CtC) had been published. The book reveals facts about the income tax long-buried in obscurity, but still fully relevant to the application of the tax.

By 2006, tens of thousands of American men and

women had learned things that enabled them to lawfully stop paying the tax, and to recover everything withheld or paid-in in connection with the tax-- Social security and Medicare contributions included. Refund checks of every penny, with interest where appropriate, were arriving daily in American mailboxes across the country from federal and state treasuries alike.

The balance of power between the state and those who learned and acted on this information began to creakily shift back toward its traditional and Constitutionally-intended relationship-- the People large and in charge, with government as their servant.

Faced with a widening and otherwise unstoppable hemorrhage in government revenue and power resulting from the spread of this previously buried information about the income tax (which they saw as a problem), the corrupt conspirators in the executive and judiciary decided to abuse the powers of their offices in an effort to suppress the inconvenient information.

INITIALLY, THESE CORRUPT ACTORS had attempted to solve their problem by pretending the inconvenient information in CtC was wrong, fit the statutory standards for "promotion of an abusive tax shelter", and could be enjoined on that basis. During the first two years the book was in print these folks brought actions toward that end in several different courts, including those of Nancy Edmunds and Victoria Roberts in the Federal District Court for the Eastern District of Michigan.

However, these contrived assaults failed. Each ended with a government motion for the dismissal of its own bogus suit. See documentation of these assaults and their collapses here.

During the course of these initial attacks on CtC, more and more Americans were receiving acknowledgements by the federal and state tax agencies of the accuracy of the book in the form of those complete refunds and in other ways, as well, such as agency surrenders on 'Notices of Deficiency', lien and levy releases, transcript entries, and so on.

— — —

NOW FOR MOST FOLKS, being repeatedly defeated in their initial series of bogus attacks on the accurate content of a book, however inconvenient that content might be to their ambitions, would be the end of the story. But some State operatives just can't abide not having their own way.

And after all, what is at stake here is trillions of dollars of wealth, and all the power that goes with it. Operatives in the State apparatus have gotten very accustomed to luxuriating in all that wealth and exercising all that power by exploiting the widespread ignorance of income tax law which the "inconvenient" revelations in CtC were curing in most everyone who read the book.

These corrupt government officials couldn't abide the thought of losing all that wealth and power and resuming the pre-1943 status of mere public servants in a governing apparatus that is a small fraction of its current bloated, arrogant, pampered and despotic size and significance. So, they stepped out into crime.

THE PERPS BEGAN THE NEW ASSAULT with a series of fraudulent claims in an unprecedented lawsuit complaint, served on the author of CtC and his wife four days before "tax day" in 2006. As its basis for being brought in the first place (something closely circumscribed under the law) the complaint asserted that the couple secured complete refunds of amounts withheld in 2002 and 2003 by catching the government napping.

The DOJ operatives responsible claimed that the government didn't know the couple had had earnings those years. They said the government wasn't really paying attention to those unique tax forms showing $0 in "wages" and thousands of dollars of withholdings, and just issued the refunds without thinking twice.

They said no official interest was piqued by the fact that the claims for refunds included Social Security and Medicare withholdings--something never before claimed or refunded in history. And they said this all happened by unconscious mistake despite the fact that these claims and refunds were made by, and to, the guy their agency had been simultaneously attempting to shut down with the bogus "abuse tax shelter promotion" assault.

Needless to say, these "validating" assertions in the government's lawsuit complaint were flat-out lies. Evidence is hardly needed to substantiate this in light of the foregoing, but see here and here.

Plainly, the returns in question were pored-over intensely, and ultimately were acknowledged as being perfectly valid and correct.

LYING ABOUT HOW THE REFUNDS WERE MADE wasn't enough, of course. There had to be an allegation of taxes owed. So, another big lie was called for.

For the fraudulent allegation that the couple had earned tax-related "income" and owed taxes, the DOJ conspirators produced what was purported to be an IRS "Examination Report" saying this, and entered it into the record of the case. But anyone who actually read the accompanying "declaration" of the anonymous "preparer" (who admitted to be using a fake name for some unexplained reason) would discover that in fact, no actual examination had been made.

So, both the assertion that the refunds were made in error and that the couple actually owed tax were fraudulent. Instead, the evidence shows that the educated filings reclaiming everything withheld and determining that no tax-relevant "income" had been received (other than the interest and dividend gains shown on the returns) were correct in every respect and actually undisputed as such.

BUT THE LIES ABOUT ERROR AND TAX LIABILITY were just the window-dressing part of the show. All the foregoing was heinous, to be sure, but the real purpose of the whole affair was in no way the mere illegal imposition of the income tax against this one couple, and the recapture of their measly $20,000.

The real purpose of the schemer's "lawsuit" was the delivery of a giant lie to the American public in order to prevent more people from reading CtC and learning the individual-empowering, state-restraining truth about the real nature and application of the income tax.

So, in addition to the fraudulent assertion that the couple's returns and claims were "false", there was another side to the "complaint", with two components. One was a mendacious assertion that CtC makes the absurd claims that "wages are not income" and that "only federal, state and local government workers are subject to the income tax". See the lies here, and the truth here.

The other "keep Americans in the dark and in the yoke" component of the conspirators' "lawsuit" ploy was a request for two unprecedented, grossly speech- conscience- and due-process-rights-violating injunctions from the court.

By one of these requested injunctions the author of CtC and his wife would be ordered to repudiate their freely-made declarations of belief concerning the taxable character of their earnings and made to instead declare-- over their own signatures-- that they believed that all their earnings are taxable. By the other, the couple would be threatened with a 'contempt-of-court" charge if they ever testified in a fashion the conspirators didn't like in a future tax-related matter (by virtue of the pretense that any disfavored testimony on a tax form would be based on the notions they had falsely ascribed to CtC).

Never before in American history have the contents of a book been the subject of a deliberate misrepresentation in a formal legal filing by government officials. Never before in American history have government officials asked a court to dictate the content of anyone's testimony, or hang a threat over anyone should they testify in ways the officials don't like in the future.

Of course, you would think that the judge presiding over this "lawsuit" with its bogus documents and assertions, and plainly lawless and unconstitutional requests would throw it out while holding her nose, and sanction, if not propose criminal charges against those responsible... Unfortunately, you'd be wrong.

Instead, Judge Nancy Edmunds joins the assault on the law and the truth, and becomes party to this monstrous crime against the American public. Without so much as a single hearing, and without ever reading CtC, she ignores the couple's demand for a jury trial and simply signs a "judgment" written entirely by the DOJ operatives.

Unsurprisingly (it having been written by the plaintiff), Edmunds' "judgment" makes "judicial findings" of every single assertion in the complaint. It also includes the rights-gutting, law-defying injunctions, as well. See them here.

NOW THE CONSPIRATORS are off to the races. National press releases are issued trumpeting CtC's "defeat in court". Government trolls begin creating websites touting the "judicial findings" and doing everything possible to spread the lies. The "tax honesty" communities on the net are infected with the lies, which therefore take hold in the alt-media community. The "tax-trouble remediation" industry is especially well-dosed with this Kool-Aid.

In every way they can think of, those behind this conspiracy have been working feverishly for years now to prevent the American public from realizing the liberating truth about the broadly-loathed but equally-broadly misunderstood income tax. They have been working equally hard to intimidate those who know the truth into relinquishing their rights to speak freely and to assert and defend their interests in legal contests over whether or not they are liable for any tax.

And yet, all the while, Americans across the country who aren't so stupid as to take on faith anything chucked-up by government officials, especially anything which, if other than how the officials portrayed it, would threaten the power and perks of those same officials, and have actually read CtC and know what it REALLY says, continue to demand and receive all their improperly-collected money back and to shut down efforts to misapply the tax to their non-federal-privilege-connected earnings.

Every single one of those now hundreds of thousands of refunds and other effective implementations of what CtC REALLY says happen only after thorough vetting by the government. Occasional resistance by the government to claims made by CtC-educated American men and women ends in government surrender to the truth.

SO, THERE YOU HAVE THE CRIME OF THE CENTURY-- which is not what's been done to Pete Hendrickson, the author of CtC, or his wife, Doreen. Those two have certainly been the victims of crimes, and these vicious crimes continue to this day (and deeply threaten the rights of every single American). But the crime of the century is not against them.

The crime of the century-- the really BIG crime-- is against YOU, and your children. It is YOU who are being deliberately and systematically lied to, for the specific purpose of keeping you in ignorant subjugation to an exploitative scheme by which corrupt elements of the political class, their cronies and their clients have been fleecing you for vast amounts of wealth throughout your entire life.

Pretty heinous, isn't it? Are you going to stand for it?

All Rights Reserved

/s/_____**John Smithton Doe**_____

John Smithton Doe (c) LS, Authorized Representative/Attorney-In-Fact for:
JOHN SMITHTON DOE
c/o Address
Zip City, State
nickname@emailaddress.net

*Subscribed To And Sworn To Before God [Titus 1:2] this XX.day of Month 20XX*

*Acknowledgement By Publication*

> Every experience is a lesson. Every loss is a gain.
>
> — Sathya Sai Baba

# AFFIDAVIT
## HOW DID WE GIVE AWAY OUR CONSENT?

STATENAME STATE    )
                              ) ss.
CountyName County  )

COMES NOW **John Smithton: Doe**, the natural living flesh and blood man, a peaceful American National on the land, under oath, who states that the following information is of his own personal knowledge, and belief.

HOW DID WE GIVE AWAY OUR CONSENT?

**TRUST AGREEMENTS**

Trust Agreements (*contracts*) are very simple. When you want to ensure that something you own or manage is taken care of while you are away (*your estate*) you can create an agreement (*a trust contract*) with a friend who will manage it for you. You set the management rules that your friend must follow in order for him to honor your agreement. This presumes 1. that you are competent to manage your estate, 2. that you own your estate, and 3. that the person you entrust to manage your estate will relinquish it back to you when you return.

The person you *entrust* with your estate is the **Trustee**, you are the **Grantor** -- and in this case the **Administrator** because you set the rules for how the trust is to be managed -- and finally, you are also the **Beneficiary** because you *benefit* from your estate being managed by your friend while you are away.

This is the *standard form* trusts take the world over,

under many names, with the *three standard roles* of a trust -- 1. **trustee**; 2. **grantor/administrator**; 3. **beneficiary**.

## Incompetence:

If you die, are lost at sea, or go crazy (*become incompetent*), the trustee can claim complete control over your estate.

Unless you *present yourself* to dispel the presumption of your incompetence or death, the trustee remains in control. The claim of your incompetence or death becomes a *cured fact in Equity Law*.

ACTION MUST BE TAKEN BY YOU to dispel the *presumption claimed* and regain control over your entrusted estate; in this case entrusted to the government.

You must be present, to indicate that you have come of age and are able to use and manage the estate entrusted to you by God (*your body, mind and soul*).

## Breach of Trust:

If the trustee *does not honor* the rules you set up, he is in BREACH OF TRUST.

In order to reclaim the trust, you must *notify him* of his failure to honor the trust agreement (*filing a UCC-1 Financing Statement is one method*.) If you *fail to notify the trustee of his breach of your trust,* you are negligent and, by definition, *incompetent.*

Clearly, if you do not recognize that the person you entrusted to managed your estate is breaking your rules, then you must not be competent. As a result, the trustee can still maintain control even *if you are alive and not lost at sea.*

**The Implied Consent of all government 'citizens':**
This is the crucial point most people overlook.

The government is the people's Trustee, and as such, Government officials must do what the people say, *or said.* If government officials CLAIM that the people want something or want something done, *and the people do not say otherwise,* the government *now has the people's* MANDATE *as a result of the people's silence, whereby silence signifies their consent.*

In other words, if the government claims that the people **volunteer to be enslaved** -- *and the people do not say otherwise and object* -- the people give their concent by inaction. Consent by inaction is called *tacit consent,* or *implied consent.*

On October 6, 1917, the Cabal controlled government, as Trustee, **declared all of its citizens to be incompetent enemies of the state.** (*See "Trading With The Enemy Act", 65th Congress, Sess. I, Cls. 105, as codified at 12 U.S.C.A. 95a*).

This claim became a **cured fact under Equity Law** when NO ONE TOOK ACTION to notify the Trustees of their Breach of Trust. As a result, the federal United States Government now has a MANDATE -- **procured from the people themselves** -- to manage the people as voluntary incompetent slaves.

**Literally,** ***we gave them our permission to do everything that has been happening on earth.***

Granted, we were unaware due to the pervasive deception on the Trustee's part, but our inability to acknowledge the fraud proves their claim of our incompetence.

The solution to this is simple, yet long of action. Before we can solve the problem, we must gain knowledge of what the problem is, how the trust relationship was set up, and where things went wrong.

**THIS IS WHAT HAPPENED:**

When you were born, your parents *unknowingly declared* you to be incompetent, and created an estate with the corporate government to manage your affairs until you come of age; become competent. *This declaration is accurate.* Until you understand how the world works, what Equity Law is, and what your true status as a Grantor and Administrator of your estate are, you are not competent.

Given that most people have no idea about any of this, the government's claim is accurate in the aggregate.

If the government were honorable, it would disclose all of this to you during the course of your lifetime and you would eventually take control of your estate.

But the Trustees are not honorable; instead they do everything they can to keep you ignorant, offering you all sorts of distractions to maintain your status of incompetency. By the time you *do come of age,* you're more interested in distractions than you are in managing your estate (*your mind, body and soul*), and taking hands-on responsibility for your life.

While you are growing up, the government *quietly*

*declares you to be dead and lost at sea.* Since you are already considered to be an enemy of the state, you can be treated as a **voluntary work slave** *under the 13th amendment.*

Many people belive that slavery ended during the Civil War with the ratification of the 13th amendment, but in fact *the 13th amendment legalized slavery on a massive scale:*

We will be discussing these treaties in more detail in a moment and how they go to the motive of *the equally bizarre and false 13th amendment* that *converts every United States of American citizen into a criminal and a slave,* or *a 14th Amendment US citizen into a piece of cargo* — being worse than a slave.

In the Equity System under the Uniform Commercial Code (UCC), our estate is created at birth via the *proof of live birth;* a birth certificate.

An Estate is an old school process meant to impart trust from the original owner, or creator, to a third party trustee. For example: During the crusades, the Crusade volunteers would entrust their estate to a family member or friend, who would manage the land for them while they were gone. If the Crusader died or was lost at sea, the friend could then claim the estate as his own. And this is exactly what the Elite claim for every birth-certificate-carrying individual in Ameria.

The United States is the only country in the world that not only condones slavery but has embedded slavery as a moral and religious right within its own Constitution.

This is exactly what the false 13th Amendment says: The 13th Amendment does not abolish slavery; it converts slavery into a claimed moral and religious right. The 13th Amendment does not end slavery; it changes the status of the slaves to that of criminals. Let me read it to you:

> "Neither slavery nor involuntary servitude, except as a punishment for crime whereof the party shall have been duly convicted, shall exist within the United States, or any place subject to their jurisdiction."

So if I can claim someone to be a criminal -- such as in summary justice -- I can then make him a slave.

How could anyone in their right mind then logically conclude that the 13th Amendment abolished slavery? It did not! It **institutionalized** slavery, to the present day, under the New World Order of the Fascist State.

Lastly, the Birth Certificate does not clearly state Live Child or Dead Child, and opens the door for a presumption of death.

Just like the family member who took ownership of the Crusader's estate, the Trustee can claim that you, the Grantor, died or was lost at sea, and so can the government, which it does.

As long as you do not *show up to say otherwise,* this presumption becomes a *'cured fact'* under Equity Law, and the government can step in and use your estate for their own purposes.

**THE SOLUTION:**

An underlying theme should now be hopefully apparent, that disclosed knowledge, or the lack there of, is the root cause and also the solution. Let's address each of the key factors.

**Our Incompetence:** Since it is true that when we are born we are not competent, *we must educate ourselves.* Knowledge is power. How can we possibly hope to get the estate we entrusted to the government back, if we don't even know that it exists, or that we have a claim to it?

The information presented in this report is a great start.

But memorizing a few facts, and filling out a UCC form is not enough; this knowledge is the first layer of the onion, and we need to go all the way to the core.

Our Estate is not a birth certificate or a piece of land somewhere, **our estate is our *mind, body and soul*** -- where its legal/lawful side merges with its spiritual side.

We must use discernment, and stop placing blind faith in leaders and experts, who **re-present** us when we should **present** ourselves; by gaining knowledge so we can see deception when it crosses our path, and call it for what it is.

In this case, **knowledge of our would-be masters** who claim to be 'consorts to God' **while in Breach of Trust with the Covenant of God,** by hiding the truth instead of sharing it; **Dark Occultism.** When we understand enough about these realities and **present** this truth to others **we are proving our competence.**

**Breach of Trust:** The trustee's of our estate, must be notified of their breach of trust. Now that we have done the work to gain knowledge, we must begin to act on this knowledge. If we continue to accept the ***illusory authority of government,*** we remain still incompetent.

For example, by voting for a president, you are entering into an agreement with the government that presumes your incompetence, and confirming their status as authority over you.

**By our very action of voting, we give them <u>our consent</u> and validate our incompetence.** In this sense, knowledge would become power, if acted upon. Either we stop consenting to all the forms of authoritarian rule (paying taxes, tickets and fines, accepting corporate justice from courts, etc) and in stopping prove our competence; or do nothing, and continue to issue implied consent. There is no grey area in this case. There are no bystanders here, either you're working to be a part of freedom, or you're working with the Cabal by staying ignorant and inactive; harsh as that may sound.

**<u>Implied Consent from all other 'citizens of government'</u>:** This last point is what unifies all the people of the world under a common cause; true freedom.

Even if we do the work of educating ourselves, and then prove our competence by acting within this knowledge in our personal lives, there is still a whole world of incompetent and willing slaves to deal with. **Because they have,** by their ignorance and inaction, **given a mandate to the governments to continue slavery and tyranny,** we cannot be islands of freedom within a sea of piracy.

Remember, their mandate is maintained by *their*

deception and *our* ignorance -- they deceive people into giving them the 'right to rule.' Our efforts MUST be focused on the unawakened ignorant masses. When enough people have dispelled their own incompetence, by gaining full knowledge of the problem, we can then act as a collective to dispel the presumed mandate of authority. Each person who is asleep is working for the Cabal and knows it not. It is our job, as ones who have learned the truth, to reveal it to them, and allow them to **become present,** so they no longer need to be **re-presented by government.**


## FINAL MESSAGE OF HOPE

The core problem is within each human being on earth, including the Cabal members themselves. They know the truth, and deceive us into accepting and maintaining our incompetence (*ignorance*). Humanity at large has been trained to be a slave race and accept authority as if real, instead of illusory. The false belief in authority must be dispelled by gaining knowledge of the truth, **that there are no real authorities, only trustee's given the power to manage our affairs, by our consent.**

As such, any solution which does not address this, is only a stopgap measure. Even if every single Cabal member were magically transported off earth, the real problem would still be here, and another Master would come in to rule the well trained incompetent slaves. As such, where we focus our time and energy is crucial. We must seek to gain mastery of ourselves, **and in doing so reclaim our estate -- our minds, bodies and souls.**

As we gain knowledge and develop mastery we become deception proof and present our competence.

Now we can look back in our lives and see how our actions helped to maintain the status quo of false authority and tyranny and begin **un-consenting** by changing ourselves. Learning about health, law, and how to be honorable will help us dispel false beliefs, and empower us with real knowledge to act competently, removing any need for a 'consort of God' to manage our lives for us.

The good news is that the whole system is designed for this purpose in the first place. Our would-be masters knew that they couldn't stay in power unless we remain ignorant and inactive. Like a magician their illusion only works if we can't see behind the stage.

The control systems many have come to loathe (*Legal codes, Equity Law, etc*) **are all based on trust agreements,** and as soon as we become aware of this, we can take action, and the whole system of control works against the Cabal, and *for us*. Now we use the UCC and Equity Law systems to our advantage, making them honorable. In this sense, these systems are a tool, like a hammer, and are not evil in and of themselves.

Simply put, the whole problem, in its full scope and impact, involves all intelligent life on earth, as each being is contributing to the current condition. We must reclaim our true estate, our minds, bodies and souls, and in so doing become the free and empowered beings we were always meant to be. Our estate is now used by us to create harmony and the long sought after Golden Age on earth, instead of the horrific NWO we seem to be headed for, today.

*All Rights Reserved*

/s/_____**John Smithton Doe**_____

John Smithton Doe (c) LS, Authorized Representative/Attorney-In-Fact for:
JOHN SMITHTON DOE
c/o Address
Zip City, State
nickname@emailaddress.net

*Subscribed To And Sworn To Before God [Titus 1:2] this XX.day of Month 20XX*

*Acknowledgement By Publication*

**Give Yourself Credit: Money Doesn't Grow On Trees! Paperback – by David E. Robinson (Author)**

http://tinyurl.com/yazcbwbt

This book honors the 77th anniversary of House Joint Resolution 192 of June 5, 1933 which Congress passed to suspend the gold standard and abrogate the gold clause of our national Constitution. Since then no one in America has been able to lawfully pay a debt. Read this book at your own risk. No money exists to pay debt. All demands for payment are demands for money. Since no money exists, all you have is your signature and your exemption number to pay a debt. Fiat Federal Reserve notes do not pay debts. Federal Reserve Notes only discharge debts. By using Federal Reserve Notes a debt is not paid, it is simply transferred to someone else -- not paid

**Commercial Law Applied: Learn To Play The Game Paperback – by David E. Robinson (Author)**

http://tinyurl.com/ycv38xcp

The principles, maxims and precepts of Commercial Law are eternal, unchanging and unchangeable. They are expressed in the Bible, both in the Old Testament and in the New. The law of commerce -- unchanged for thousands of years -- forms the underlying foundation of all law on this planet; and for governments around the world. It is the law of nations, and of everything that human civilization is built upon. This is why Commercial Law is so powerful. When you operate at the level of Commercial Law, by these precepts, nothing that is of inferior statute can overturn or change it, or abrogate it, or meddle with it. It is the fundamental source of all authority, power and functional reality.

**Hardcore Redemption-in-Law: Commercial Freedom & Release Paperback – by David E. Robinson (Author)**

http://tinyurl.com/y95ujsq6

"And the serpent case out of his mouth water as a flood after the woman and went to make war with her . . . to devour her." -- Revelation 12:15-17 and 12:4. The Endtime Beast is a system of law borrowed from the law of the sea implemented inland so that the "ecclesia" (the remnant) are forced into earnest demonstration. This system of law is patterned after the maritime trust that transfers the commercial interests of the people, called "suretyship," to alien strangers wherein commerce knows no bounds and is typified by a flood. The woman is non other than the real true bona fide seed of Abraham, Isaac, and Jacob -- their progeny of today.


**Be The One: To Execute Your Trust Paperback – by David E. Robinson (Author)**

http://tinyurl.com/yaynrokz

Presumptions? or Facts! The State operates on presumptions. Courts operate on presumptions. But what binds me to their presumptions? Where's the contract? What obligations in the contract am I allegedly bound to perform? Did I agree to it? Was the contract valid? Was mutual consideration exchanged? What type of consideration was exchanged? What is in the contract that I am supposed to perform? Was I aware of the contract? Was the contract fully disclosed? Did I sign the contract with my autograph in ink? Statutory laws are public servant codes for society's slaves; for agents of government. We're all presumed to be employees and servants of the state. But, we're servants of God instead; students of the earth, charged with its cultivation and care.

# 10 MAXIMS OF LAW

1. A workman is worthy of his hire.

2. All men are equal under the law.

3. In commerce truth is sovereign.

4. Truth is expressed in the form of an affidavit.

5. An unrebutted affidavit stands as truth in commerce.

6. An unrebutted affidavit becomes judgement in commerce.

7. A matter must be expressed to be resolved.

8. He who leaves the field of battle first loses by default.

9. Sacrifice is the measure of credibility.

10. A lien or claim can be satisfied only through rebuttal by counter affidavit point by point, resolution by a jury, or payment of the claim.

Printed in Great Britain
by Amazon